FOUR ESSENTIAL BUDDHIST COMMENTARIES

by

His Holiness the XIVth Dalai Lama

LIBRARY OF TIBETAN WORKS AND ARCHIVES

Reprints: 1993, 2001, 2005

ISBN: 81-85102-20-1

Published by the Library of Tibetan Works & Archives, Dharamsala, Distt. Kangra, H.P., India, and printed at Indraprastha Press (CBT), Nehru House, 4 Bahadur Shah Zafar Marg, New Delhi.

Contents

Publisher's Note

We are happy to bring forth *Four Essential Buddhist Commentaries,* a bi-lingual dharma work comprising important commentaries provided by His Holiness the Dalai Lama of Tibet on four noted Tibetan Buddhist texts by Thogs-med bzang-po, Tsong-Khapa, Geshe Langri Thangpa and the Seventh Dalai Lama.

Rendered into English by a number of Western and Tibetan translators, we are sure the readers will derive spiritual guidance and strength from these concise and clear commentaries provided by one of the most significant Buddhist leaders of our time.

Publication Department
Library of Tibetan Works & Archives

May, 1982

The Thirty-Seven Practices of All Buddhas' Sons (*rGyal-sras lag-len so-bdun-ma*)

by Thogme Zangpo

Translated by: Geshe Ngawang Dhargyey, SharpaTulku, KhamlunTulku, Alexander Berzin and Jonathan Landaw.

I pay heartfelt homage to you, Lokeshvara;
You have true compassion extending to all.

To those who in every coming and going
Have seen that each thing is inherently void,
And thus can devote both their time and their efforts
With one aim in mind—"Let me benefit all!"
To such foremost Gurus and you, Lokeshvara,
All-seeing protector, with utmost respect
I bow down before you in constant obeisance,
And turn to your service my thoughts, words and deeds.

The Fully Enlightened Victorious Buddhas,
From whom all true pleasure and benefits derive,
Have reached their attainment by following Dharma
And leading their lives through this noblest of paths.
To live by the Dharma depends on full knowledge
Of how we must practice and what we must do,
Thus I'll attempt now a brief explanation
Of what is the practice of all Buddhas' Sons.

(1)

This sound human body endowed with full leisure—
An excellent vessel rare to be found—
Since now we've obtained one in no way deficient,
Let's work night and day without veering off course
To take across the ocean and free from samsara
Not only ourselves but all others as well.
First listen, think hard, then do much meditation—
The Sons of the Buddhas all practice this way.

(2)

Remaining too long in one place our attraction
To loved ones upsets us, we're tossed in its wake.
The flames of our anger towards those who annoy us
Consume what good merit we've gained in the past.
The darkness of closed-minded thought dims our outlook,
We lose vivid sight of what's right and what's wrong.
We must give up our home and set forth from our country—
The Sons of the Buddhas all practice this way.

(3)

Withdrawing completely from things that excite us,
Our mental disturbances slowly decline.
And ridding our mind of directionless wandering,
Attention on virtue will surely increase.
As wisdom shines clearer, the world comes in focus,
Our confidence grows in the Dharma we've learned.
Live all alone far away in seclusion—
The Sons of the Buddhas all practice this way.

(4)

Regardless of how long we spent living together,
Good friends and relations must some day depart.
Our wealth and possessions collected with effort
Are left far behind at the end of our life.

Our mind, but a guest in our body's great guest house,
Must vacate one day and travel beyond—
Cast away thoughts that concerns but this lifetime—
The Sons of the Buddhas all practice this way.

(5)

From staying together with friends who misguide us,
Our hatred, desires and ignorance grow.
With little time left to continue our studies,
We don't think of Dharma; we meditate less.
Our love and compassion for all sentient beings
Are lost and forgotten while under their sway.
Sever such ties with misleading companions—
The Sons of the Buddhas all practice this way.

(6)

When placing ourself in the hands of a Guru,
We're turning sincerely for guidance to someone
Whose competence both in the scriptures and practice
Expands like the moon growing full.
We'll then solve all our problems, dispel our delusion,
If we place our full confidence solely in him.
We must cherish our Guru far more than our body—
The Sons of the Buddhas all practice this way.

(7)

The gods of this world are not yet free from sorrow,
For caught in samsara, some day they must fall.
If they're bound as we are, how can they protect us?
How can someone in prison free anyone else?
But Buddha, his teachings and those who live by them
Are free to give comfort—they'll not let us down.
Go to the Three Jewels of Refuge for shelter—
The Sons of the Buddhas all practice this way.

(8)

Buddha has said that the grief past endurance
Of creatures whose lives contain nothing but pain
Is unfortunate fruit of the wrongs they've committed
Against other beings in lifetime gone by.
Not wishing to suffer from horrible torment,
Not flinching if even our life is at stake,
Turn from all actions that harm other beings—
The Sons of the Buddhas all practice this way.

(9)

Like the dew that remains for a moment or two
On the tips of the grass and then melts with the dawn,
The pleasures we find in the course of our lives
Last only an instant, they cannot endure;
While the freedom we gain when becoming a Buddha
Is a blissful attainment not subject to change.
Aim every effort to this wondrous achievement—
The Sons of the Buddhas all practice this way.

(10)

In each incarnation, through all of our lives,
We've been cared for by others with motherly love.
While these mothers of ours are still lost in samsara,
How cruel to ignore them and free but ourself!
To save other beings, though countless in number,
To free from their sorrow these mothers of old,
Produce Bodhichitta, the wish to be Buddha—
The Sons of the Buddhas all practice this way.

(11)

All of our sufferings, without an exception,
Derive from the wish to please but ourselves;
While the thoughts and the actions that benefit others
Conceive and give birth to supreme Buddhahood.

Thus in exchange for our selfish desires
And shameful neglect of our suffering kin,
Replace thoughts of self with concern for all others—
The Sons of the Buddhas all practice this way.

(12)

If under the sway of compulsive desire
And longing for things that he does not possess,
Some unfortunate person has stolen our riches
Or lets others rob us and idly stands by;
Then out of compassion and with no attachment,
To him we must dedicate all of our prayers:
May he have wealth, our body and merits—
The Sons of the Buddhas all practice this way.

(13)

Although we're not guilty of any offence
And never have harmed anyone in our life
If someone deluded should threaten to kill us
Because he is crazed with a tormented mind,
Then mercifully wishing for him not to suffer
Further misfortune because of his state,
Selflessly take on the effects of his actions—
The Sons of the Buddhas all practice this way.

(14)

If someone insulting should spread ugly rumours
About us with cruel words unpleasant to hear,
And even if what he has said spreads to others
And gains wide acceptance as being the truth;
Yet out of our wish for the one who's maligned us
To conquer his trouble and gain peace of mind,
Praise all his virtues and treat him with kindness—
The Sons of the Buddhas all practice this way.

(15)

If in the midst of a large crowd of people
Someone should single us out for abuse,
Exposing our faults before all within hearing
And pointing out clearly the flaws we still have;
Then not getting angry nor being defensive,
Just listening in silence and heeding his words,
Bow in respect to this man as our teacher—
The Sons of the Buddhas all practice this way.

(16)

If someone we love and have cared for with kindness,
As an unselfish mother would cherish her child,
Should shun our devotion with thankless resentment
And treat us as if we're his most hated foe,
Then seeing these acts as a terrible sickness
Befallen our child and affecting his mind,
Treat him with even more love and affection—
The Sons of the Buddhas all practice this way.

(17)

If by our own equals or those who are lower
In intellect, spiritual level, or wealth,
We're insulted and treated as if we were nothing
By force of their pride and their jealous contempt,
Then seeing that they are like Gurus to teach us
To always be humble and conquer our pride,
Treat them with honour and place them above us—
The Sons of the Buddhas all practice this way.

(18)

If we are but men of most meagre subsistence
And always receive a great deal of abuse,
If we find ourselves constantly gripped by much sickness
And experience harm, interruptions and pain,

Then accepting ourself all these hardships which others
Would surely have suffered from the wrongs they had done,
Never lose courage to take pain from others—
The Sons of the Buddhas all practice this way.

(19)

Though praised and well-known, admired by many
Who act most respectful by bowing their head,
Though having obtained a vast treasure of riches
Which equals the store of the great God of Wealth,
Yet seeing full well that this fruit of samsara,
Though fortunate, still has no essence at all,
Cast out what pride we might have in these glories—
The Sons of the Buddhas all practice this way.

(20)

If anger that dwells in our heart lies neglected
And, turning instead to our external foes,
We try to destroy them and even kill thousands,
The thousands of others will plague us still more,
So seeing this action is not the solution,
Let us muster the forces of mercy and love;
Turn inwards and tame the wild flow of our mind-stream—
The Sons of the Buddhas all practice this way.

(21)

Indulging in objects our senses run after
And drinking salt water are one and the same:
The more we partake, for our own satisfaction,
The more our desire and thirst for them grow.
Thus when we conceive a compulsive attraction
Towards whatever object our senses desires,
Abandon it quickly without hesitation—
The Sons of the Buddhas all practice this way.

(22)

Whatever appears to be truly existent
Is merely what mind in delusion creates;
This mind of ours also is from the beginning
Devoid of an essence inherently real.
Then realizing Truth is beyond the conceptions
We have of the known and the knower as well,
Dispel the belief in inherent existence—
The Sons of the Buddhas all practice this way.

(23)

Whenever we meet with a beautiful object,
Or something attractive which pleases our mind,
Do not be deceived into thinking it differs
In fact from a summertime rainbow:
Though both of them have such a lovely appearance,
Nothing substantial lies behind their facade.
Abandon the drives of compulsive attraction—
The Sons of the Buddhas all practice this way.

(24)

The various ills in our life that we suffer
Resemble the death of our son in a dream;
To hold as the truth what is merely illusion
Is needless exhaustion of body and mind.
For this very reason, when faced with unpleasant
Conditions that normally cause us much grief,
Approach them as if they were only illusion—
The Sons of the Buddhas all practice this way.

(25)

The beings who strive to be Fully Enlightened
Would give up their body pursuing this aim;
With this peerless example, what need is the mention
Of gifts we should make of the objects we own.

Without any hope of return for our kindness.
Not considering even the merit to be gained,
Engage in the practice of generous giving—
The Sons of the Buddhas all practice this way.

(26)

If lacking strict moral control of our conduct
We haven't been able to reach our own goal,
How can we fulfil all the wishes of others?
Undisciplined effort is surely absurd!
We first must renounce our attachment to pleasure
Which binds us so tightly to samsara's wheel,
Then protect all our vows of sworn moral behaviour—
The Sons of the Buddhas all practice this way.

(27)

For all Bodhisattvas with minds set on merit
Who wish to amass a great store of good deeds,
Encounters with those causing harm and destruction
Which test their commitment are mines of great wealth.
For this very reason, abandon resentment
And anger directed towards those who do harm;
Perfect meditation on patient endurance—
The Sons of the Buddhas all practice this way.

(28)

If Sravakas as well as Pratyekabuddhas,
Who work towards Nirvana for merely themselves,
Exert so much effort fulfilling their purpose
That were they in flames, they'd not stray from their goal,
Then how much more energy must be expended
By those of us working for everyones sake;
Enlightenment calls for the most perseverance—
The Sons of the Buddhas all practice this way.

(29)

Higher insight that penetrates right to the essence,
Revealing the true way in which things exist,
Can only root out our emotional problems
If mental quiescence is laid as its base.
Thus surpassing the four formless states of absorption
We must work to achieve single-minded control,
And the full concentration of deep meditation—
The Sons of the Buddhas all practice this way.

(30)

Perfection of Charity, patience and morals,
Absorption and effort alone won't suffice;
Without the Perfection of Wisdom these five are
Unable to bring us to full Buddhahood.
With the methods of pure Bodhichitta develop
The wisdom to see that the actor, the act,
And the acted upon lack inherent existence—
The Sons of the Buddhas all practice this way.

(31)

Without making efforts to analyze clearly
Delusions we have and mistakes we commit,
Then even though outwardly practicing Dharma,
We still may perform many non-Dharmic deeds.
For this very reason, let's try to examine
Mistakes and delusions, the faults we possess,
Then afterwards try to remove them completely—
The Sons of the Buddhas all practice this way.

(32)

While speaking of others, the force of delusion
May cause us to dwell on the flaws they possess;
Should those we find fault with be Bodhisattvas,
Our own reputation will suffer instead.

So avoid the mistake of disparaging others
Who've entered upon Mahayana's great path;
Only the faults that we have should we mention—
The Sons of the Buddhas all practice this way.

(33)

Domestic disputes with our friends and relations,
To gain their respect or the things we feel due,
Will leave us unable to listen to Dharma:
Unable to study or meditate well.
Since danger is found in the homes of our patrons,
As well as in those of our family and friends,
Abandon attachment we have to these households—
The Sons of the Buddhas all practice this way.

(34)

The words of abuse that we utter in anger
Cause others much pain by disturbing their mind;
And we who are striving to be Bodhisattvas
Will find that our practice will surely decline.
So seeing the faults that arise from harsh language,
Which those who must hear find unpleasant and rude,
Abandon abuse directed towards others—
The Sons of the Buddhas all practice this way.

(35)

Defiled types of actions will soon become habits
As we grow accustomed to base states of mind;
Strenuous effort will then be required
For the force of opponents to counter these stains.
So armed with the weapons alertness and memory,
Attack such defilements as lust on first sight;
Remove these obstructions that hinder our progress—
The Sons of the Buddhas all practice this way.

(36)

In short then, whatever we do in whatever
Condition or circumstance we may confront,
Should be done with the force of complete self-awareness
Which comprehends fully the state of our mind.
Then always possessing alertness and memory,
Which keep us in focus and ready to serve,
We must work for the welfare of all sentient beings—
The Sons of the Buddhas all practice this way.

(37)

All merits we gain from the efforts we're making
To put into practice these virtuous ways,
Which we do for the sake of removing the suffering
Endured by the limitless mothers we've had,
We must dedicate purely for them to be Buddhas,
With wisdom which sees that both they and ourself,
As well as this merit all lack true existence—
The Sons of the Buddhas all practice this way.
By carefully following all of the teachings
My most holy Gurus have imparted to me –
Concerning the meanings of sutra and tantra
Explained by the Buddhas and masters of old
I have written this work on the practices numbering
Thirty and seven of all Buddhas' Sons
To benefit those who desire to follow
The path that all Sons of Buddhas must tread.

Because of my poor intellectual powers
And the meagre amount of training I've had,
I haven't been able to write polished verses
In metre and style which would please those with skill;
But as I've relied on the words of the sutras
And all that my most holy Gurus have taught,

I am certain that this is without any errors;
This truly is what Buddhas' Sons have all done.

However, because the extent and the depth
Of the great waves of conduct of all Buddha's Sons
Are hard to be fathomed by someone of limited
Power of intellect as is myself,
There are bound to be faults, contradictions in meaning,
Disjointed connections and many such flaws;
So most holy Gurus, I beg your indulgence,
Be patient with all the shortcomings I have.

With pure Bodhicitta of ultimate Voidness,
Yet relative nature of mercy and love,
Devoid of extremes of this worldly existence
And passive absorption in blissful release,
May all sentient beings receiving the merit
Amassed by the effort I've made in this work
Soon reach your attainment, O great Lokeshvara,
All-seeing protector with love for us all.

The Three Principal Aspects of the Path

By Je Tsong-Khapa

Translated by Tsepak Rigzin

Obeisance to the venerable Gurus.

I will explain as I am able accordingly,
The essential meanings of all the teachings of the victor,
The path proclaimed by all supreme sons of the victor,
And the passage for those fortunate ones wishing liberation.

Listen with clear mind those fortunate ones,
Whoever is not attached to the joys of cyclic existence,
But endeavors for a meaningful (life) of leisures and endowments,
Directing your mind towards the path pleasing the victors.

Without pure renunciation, there is no means to pacify
Attraction to the pleasurable effects of the ocean of (cyclic) existence.
For attachment to (cyclic) existence completely binds all beings,
Therefore, seek renunciation at the beginning.

Familiarizing your mind with leisures and endowments
That are difficult to find,
And that life has no time to waste,
You reverse the allurements of this life.
Contemplating again and again the unfailing effect of Karma
And the sufferings of the cyclic existence,

You reverse the allurements of future lives.

Having meditated thus, when you do not generate even for an instant,
An admiration for the prosperity of cyclic existence,
But an attitude of seeking liberation, throughout day and night,
At that moment you have generated the renunciation.

If this renunciation is not conjoined
With the pure Bodhi-mind,
It will not become a cause for the perfect bliss
Of the highest Bodhi.
Thus the wise ones must generate the supreme Bodhi.

Sentient beings are carried away
By the current of the four violent rivers,
Tied by the tight bounds of Karma, difficult to undo,
And are caught in the iron cage of grasping at (independent) self,
Thoroughly enveloped by the thick darkness of ignorance.

Sentient beings are born in the boundless cyclic existence,
And in (their) rebirths are continuously tormented
By the three sufferings.
Contemplating this state of mothers,
Generate the supreme (Bodhi) mind.

If you lack the wisdom realizing the mode of existence,
Even though you have familiarized yourself
With renunciation and Bodhi-mind,
The root of cyclic existence cannot be cut.
Therefore, strive to realize the dependent arising.

Whoever, sees the ever unfailing (nature) of the cause and effect,
Of all the phenomena of cyclic existence and beyond,

And thoroughly destroys the mode of misapprehension,
He has entered the path pleasing the Buddhas.

So long as, the two understandings:
The unfailing (nature) of appearances--the dependent arising,
And the emptiness--lacking assertion of (independent existence),
Appears as separate, still,
He has not realized the thought of the Muni.

When the (two realizations) exist simultaneously without alteration,
Merely from seeing the dependent arising as unfailing,
And, if the ascertained understanding of (non-inherent existence)
Destroys all modes of misapprehension of objects,
At that time the analysis of the view of (emptiness) is complete.

Further, the extreme of existence is avoided by the appearances,
And the extreme of non-existence is avoided by the emptiness.
If, (from the sphere) of emptiness, the mode of arising
Of the cause and effect is known.
You will not be captivated by the extreme views.

Thus when you have realized accordingly,
The essentials of the three principal aspects of the path,
Seek solitude and generate the power of effort,
And quickly accomplish the final goal, dear son.

This instruction was given by Je Tsong-Khapa to his disciple Ngawang Dakpa, a relative of the king of Gyalrong Tshakho.

Commentary on "Thirty-Seven Bodhisattva Practices" and "The Three Principal Aspects of the Path"

His Holiness the XIVth Dalai Lama

Translated and condensed by Alexander Berzin

Day One

Many people are here today from various different places, even Tibet, and you have all come for the Dharma purpose of listening to teachings. Therefore, concerning the development of Bodhichitta and so forth, I shall teach here in Bodh Gaya the "Thirty-Seven Bodhisattva Practices" by Thogmey Zangpo and also "The Three Principle Paths" by Je Tsong-Khapa. As we are in a very holy place, the merit collected here is much more powerful than elsewhere. But for this merit to be most effective we must have a very widespread and extensive motivation and attitude. This is necessary not only for the listeners to the teachings, but for the Lama or Guru as well.

The Enlightened Being, the Buddha, the Compassionate One, has a body with 32 major and 80 minor features and a faculty of speech with 60 perfect characteristics. Furthermore his mind is free from all delusions and obstacles such that he always has bare perception of Voidness and all phenomena exactly as they are. Such a compassionate, Fully Perfected Buddha demonstrated his Enlightenment here in Bodh Gaya 2,500 years ago and we are all in this very place now.

The times at present are very difficult with many wars, famines, disasters and so on. Nevertheless, due to our previously collected merit, we have been born at such a time and place and, even under such trying conditions, have had the precious opportunity to encounter the teachings and meet with Gurus. Therefore, as much as we can, we should try to practice what we hear. Simply praying to receive something, however, cannot be considered Dharma. The Dharma, rather, is something we ourselves must personally put into action. It is not just taking refuge by our mouth's reciting some words, but rather implementing into our daily behavior what we say. Thus we should take a keen interest in the teachings and involve ourselves with their combined study and practice. But first it is necessary to know how to do this.

Dharma is something that the more we engage in, the happier we become. This occurs as a result of our collection of merit from the various virtuous actions we perform. This is the reason then why we should not be followers of the Buddha just by our mouths, but rather by our practice. It will create more happiness. Thus while here in Bodh Gaya where we have the opportunity of meeting with the Dharma, and especially with the Mahayana Dharma, it is important to try to collect as much merit as possible. Most critical for this is to set a proper motivation. If we have a widespread and very positive one, there is great benefit to be gained. But if we practice without such a motivation, it will not be as effective and that will never do.

For the Lama also it must be the same. The Lama must teach not out of pride or in order to gain fame and respect, nor out of jealousy, or a wish to compete with others. Rather, his sole motivation must be to benefit others as much as he can, respecting everyone here, all beings, without condescendingly looking down upon any. The audience also should not be prideful, but should listen attentively and respectfully to receive the precious teachings of the Buddha. If both the Lama and the disciples behave properly and carefully in this way, it is extremely beneficial and we can all collect some merit.

No matter what delusions we have, it is necessary to apply remedies to them and not be discouraged. In so doing, then very slowly we will be able to resolve our problems and be rid of them. We will find that gradually we improve each year. Since the mind by nature is not stained by these delusions, we can succeed if we set our mind to cleaning itself. As the suffering we experience is due to our mind's not being disciplined or tamed, this is what we must remedy. But it will not come about all at once. For example, if we are trying to make a very wild and unruly person more peaceful and cultivated, we can only succeed slowly and gradually over many, many years. The same is true with our mind. Although we have faults, we can slowly improve. We can see a similar phenomenon with children. At first they do not know anything; they are completely uneducated. But they go through the various classes at school, the first grade, second and so on, and eventually through this gradual process they learn and become educated. The same is true when we build a house, we do it storey by storey, floor by floor. We do it gradually without worrying about how long it will take, and just progress straightforwardly through the various stages involved until we complete the task. We should apply this same attitude when dealing with our mind.

As for setting our motivation, we should try to do this as best as we can, at our own level, and slowly we will be able to improve it through stages as described in the "Lam-rim" or "Graded Path". Most of you know about this, but for the new people here I shall explain a little. To practice Dharma, then, is not a process of simply changing clothes, status or the amount of wealth we have. Rather it means to change our attitudes and tame our own mind. No matter who we might be—even myself, the Dalai Lama—I cannot be considered a Dharma person unless my mind is tamed. And we can never say someone has such a mind simply because of the name he has or the clothes he wears, but only because of his actual mental condition. Therefore the most important and crucial point is to tame our mind.

All of you here should examine yourselves. All of us want happiness and nobody wishes to suffer. There is not one of us who, if we have a headache, does not wish to be rid of it. Isn't that so? This is true of both physical and mental pain. But many stages are involved in eliminating unwanted suffering and obtaining desired happiness. It is not something that happens all at once. Even in trying to help or tame an animal and bring it some happiness, we have to do it in stages suited to that particular beast. For instance, first we try to feed it, we refrain from frightening it, mistreating it and so forth. Likewise the same applies to us, we have to help ourselves by stages.

First we try to think in terms of benefiting ourselves for this coming year, or for the next year. Then eventually we increase our scope to think in terms of twenty years ahead and then may be to try to gain a human rebirth for our next lifetime, hoping to gain happiness and not to have suffering on a more long-term basis. We progress through such stages. Therefore, now that we are human beings, it is very important to think ahead and not to do so just on a temporary, superficial level, but to try to attain ultimate happiness.

In our more usual pursuit of happiness we seek food, clothing, shelter and so forth for our body. But the reason for being a human is not just that. Even if we are rich we find that wealthy people can still have a great deal of mental suffering. We can see this very clearly in the West. There are many people who have much money and physical comfort, however they also have numerous mental problems such as depression, unclear minds and various miserable states. In fact, we find a lot of people there taking drugs and medicine to try to improve this state. This demonstrates that even though they have material comfort and wealth, they want mental happiness above all and in addition to their physical pleasures, and that wealth alone does not bring both. Even if we are very healthy and strong, if our mind is unhappy this will not be enough. Therefore, we need both physical and mental happiness. Of these the mind is more important, since it rules us. Therefore the emphasis should be on bringing about happiness of the mind.

But what brings about this happiness of mind? It comes through the channel of our thoughts. If we do not use our mind and think, we will not be able to bring ourselves happiness. It works both ways. For instance, no matter what delusions are our strongest, whether it be anger, desire, pride, jealousy or whatever, the more we think about them, the more we act on them, and the more suffering we have. If anger, for instance, is our strongest delusion, then the more angry we become, the more unhappy we are. If we are bitter and angry about Tibet, for instance, are we happy or unhappy? We are unhappy, it is very clear. Therefore as an opponent if we think about love and compassion, this counters our anger and brings about peace of mind. Thus a good heart and kind thoughts bring us happiness. As all of us want this happiness and wish to eliminate our sufferings, we should try to see that the root of this is the mind.

In short, the stronger our attachment and aversion are, the stronger our suffering will be. The weaker these are, the happier we will be. Thus, we should think about what we need to eliminate, what we need to abandon. If we are very jealous, for instance, what happens? All of us must die in the end, so we will never be able to retain the aims of our jealousy. As we will never be able to satisfy completely our jealous desires, we will never be happy so long as we are jealous. The same is true with pride. No one can stay in the same condition forever, we cannot always remain young and youthful. Whatever we are proud of, we will eventually lose. Thus pride as well is a very unhappy state of mind. If we are in a restaurant, for instance, and are jealous of the good meal that someone else is eating, what does this bring us? It brings us only unhappiness, it certainly does not fill our stomach!

If we think of ourselves, the Tibetans, if we feel angry and jealous of the Chinese, are we happy like that? Is that a happy state of mind? It definitely is not. Think of somebody whose main activity of life is to act out his attachments and aversions. Such a person may become very powerful, very famous, he can even go down in history. But what has such a person attained? He has merely attained his name's going down in history. He has not become happy, he is dead. So if we spend our entire life practicing delusions, no matter how wealthy and powerful we become, this will not bring us happiness.

If we think about our situation these days in Bodh Gaya, for instance, we can understand this even more clearly. Even with the Dalai Lama here, if you are in such a holy place and become angry with a beggar or angry with the difficult physical conditions, are you happy at that moment? On the other hand, when your delusions are weaker and you are doing something virtuous here, are you happy then? Think about it. Your state of mind even affects your neighbours, friends and children. Consider a family situation, for instance. If you are very angry and become cross with your children, you hit them, they cry—it makes everybody unhappy, doesn't it? But if you are not angry, if you are very relaxed, then you let the children play and everybody is very happy and peaceful. In a country also we find that if detachment and tolerance are widely practiced, then everyone shares in the happiness of that place. This holds true for individual people, families and for countries. The more delusions there are, the more unhappiness there is, whereas the less the delusions, the more the happiness.

As for myself, I think quite a bit about the drawbacks of the delusions, all the bad things that they bring me, and also the advantages of not having any. This helps me very much in putting the emphasis in my own life on having less delusions. Then as a bonus we find that we are able to enjoy life more, our food tastes better and everything goes very nicely. But if our mind is filled with delusions, then even if we are doing meditations, recitations or whatever, we will not derive any happiness from them at all. Therefore we should always try to think of how disadvantageous the delusions are.

In short, if our mind is tamed and we have no delusions, then we become very happy. Therefore the best thing that can happen as a result of taming our mind is that delusions will not arise at all. But even if they should come up, the next best thing we find is that we no longer act them out. For instance, it is best if we never become angry at all, but should our temper flare up, we find that if we have tamed our mind, we will not act it out. We will not punch someone in the face, for instance, or call him a bad name, or have any such crude reaction.

Thus slowly, over a gradual process, we find that the opponents become stronger and stronger, our mind becomes more and more tamed and in this way we become happier. As beginners, therefore, we should try never to have our delusions of anger, attachment and so forth arise. But even if they do, we should try to not act them out. Do you understand? If we tame our mind this is a Dharma practice, but if we do not, then it is not Dharma. If we eliminate the delusions altogether, we attain a state of cessation or peace and this is in fact the actual Dharma.

There are Four Noble Truths: true sufferings, their true origins, true cessation and true paths. For true sufferings, we can think of the various types of unhappiness, of death, sickness, old age and so forth. The Buddha said it is very important to be aware of suffering, and what is the root of this suffering?

The root is an untamed mind, and more specifically, it is the delusions. Therefore the delusions are said to be true origins or causes of suffering, as are the karmic impulses that arise under the power of these delusions. Thus it is delusions and karma that are true causes of suffering. Therefore, as all of us do not wish for any suffering and want only to eliminate it, we should see that the cause of this suffering is our having an untamed mind. Since we want to bring about a cessation of that suffering, what we must do then is cause our delusions to cease into the Dharmadhatu or sphere of Voidness. This is known as a Nirvana of true cessation.

As there are many stages in the process of abandoning the delusions, or causing them to cease, this process entails what is known as the true paths of the Aryas or Noble Ones. More precisely, since during the process of eliminating the various delusions, we also work to attain more and more good qualities, the elimination of delusions and faults on the one side and the attainment of good qualities on the other are known as true paths. In short, there is suffering, it has a cause, we wish for its cessation and to enact this, we need to follow a path. The result of this is then a definite cessation, peace, or a state of Nirvana, the State Beyond Sorrow, and this brings us lasting happiness. This is what the Buddha demonstrated here in Bodh Gaya by his example and afterwards he taught the Four Noble Truths. The first two then, true sufferings and their origins, are on the deluded suffering side, and the second two, true cessations and paths, are on the liberating or pure side.

We can see then that the motivation for Dharma practice is not like, for instance, when a child listens to a parent and does what he is told simply because the parent has told him to do that. Engaging in Dharma should not be just obeying the words of a parent like an obedient child. Rather, we engage in dharma practice because we wish to eliminate our own suffering and for that reason we follow the instructions of what a teacher tells us to do in order to tame our own mind. Do you understand?

Many factors are involved in eliminating suffering. For instance, there are the sufferings of hunger, cold and so forth and for eliminating each of these we would rely on different types of methods or work. Thus through the work of farmers, merchants and so forth, we can eliminate our hunger and cold. For the suffering of sickness we would rely on doctors and medicine. But these are only temporary aids, not ultimate cures. If we are sick, we can take medicine and pills to make us strong, but these will not eliminate our old age and death. In short, we cannot obtain the ultimate elimination of these sufferings of birth, sickness, old age and death, by ordinary means, even if some methods can bring us temporary relief.

Many religions, such as some of the Hindu sects, Christianity and so forth, accept a God who is the creator of happiness and suffering. If we pray to this God, he will grant us happiness. But this is not how Buddha explained. Buddha said that our suffering and happiness are not in God's hands, but solely in our own. Unlike these religions which accept only one Jewel of Refuge, namely God, we accept Three Jewels. Buddha is the one who shows the path of what is to be accepted and what is to be rejected. Therefore Buddha is like a teacher and not a creator God. Our karma or behaviour is what creates our happiness and suffering. Happiness comes from positive or virtuous actions. Therefore we should try to act in this way as much as we can. On the other hand, since unhappiness comes from negative actions, we should try to eliminate them as much as possible. What Buddha taught then was the path of cause and effect. Our fate is in our hands, not God's nor, for that matter, in Buddha's. Thus, the actual refuge is in the Dharma, which is something we must develop on our own mindstream. In other words, by eliminating the delusions and so forth from our own mind, we will eliminate our suffering and attain happiness. In addition, in order to develop this Dharma Refuge on our own mindstream, we need helpers to provide an example and assist in this process. Such people are known as the Sangha Refuge. In short, then, the Buddha shows the refuge, the Dharma is the actual refuge and the Sangha community helps set the example. There is no one single God or Jewel of Refuge that is going to give us happiness and eliminate our suffering.

In English "religion" is often used as a word for translating the Tibetan term for Dharma, and this word "religion" has the connotation of a system in which a Creator God is accepted. Therefore it is commonly said that Buddhism is atheistic, and not really a religion. The Chinese, however, say that they are atheists, that the Buddhists are religious and that Buddhism is a religion. But actually by the above definition we are atheists too. Furthermore, we accept the words of the Buddha not on blind faith, but only after we have examined them carefully. If they are reasonable we accept them and if not then we don't. For instance, we have many logical proofs for phenomena such as rebirth and only after we have examined the issue can we accept it. If something can be established by logic then it is acceptable. But if it is only based on blind faith, that will never do. Therefore do not just say "I believe". The main point is to analyze by logic and reason. If something is not in accord with reason and reality, do not accept it. We must always base our beliefs on reasoning.

When Buddha spoke in the past, he gave the complete teachings. There is no need to revise what he said, add to it or improve it. It is just a matter of us practicing what Buddha preached. It is not very complicated. We can understand this from the example of medicine. Doctors examine individual patients and then prescribe the medicine suited to each. If the treatment does not work, only a fool would say that the fault lies with the science of medicine. A smart person would realize that the reason the medicine did not work for him is because of the medical practitioner, and not because of the science of medicine itself. Likewise the same is true with Buddhism. There are no faults in the "Tripitaka" or "Three Baskets", the texts of Buddha's direct teachings. If we examine, we will see that the confusion does not lie in the sources themselves. Therefore what we must do is practice properly as is stated in these various sources. Do you understand?

The main practice then is taming the mind. For this we must hear teachings and to do this properly we need a correct motivation. Buddha gave both Hinayana and Mahayana teachings. The main point in mind in the Mahayana is helping others. In Hinayana, the emphasis is that even if we cannot help others, we should at least not harm them. Thus the emphasis in both is on how to help and be of benefit to others. We must learn from this. If we can help others, we should do so, and if we cannot then certainly we should never harm them. It never says anywhere that we should become angry with anyone, does it?

In the Mahayana teachings it also says we should try to ignore our own selfish purposes and work for the sake of the masses of others. This is the Buddhist message, isn't it? Thus we need to have a pure, warm and kind heart. We should try then to set a Bodhichitta motivation to work to attain Enlightenment in order to be able to benefit all beings, and with such a motivation listen to 'Thirty-Seven Bodhisattva Practices" as written here by the Bodhisattva Thogmey Zangpo.

Thogmey Zangpo lived at the time of Buton Rinpoche, which was two generations before Je Tsong-Khapa. He was a Lama mostly trained in the Sakya tradition and from an early age was famous for being primarily interested in helping others. As a child, for instance, he would even become cross at people if they did not help others. Gradually he became a monk, devoting himself to various Lamas, mostly two specific teachers. He practiced both sutra and tantra and became a very learned, realized practitioner. He was most famous for his development of Bodhichitta and this was done mostly through the teachings on the equalizing and exchanging of self with others. In fact, if we try to think of a Bodhisattva, Thogmey Zangpo is one who comes to mind immediately as an example, doesn't he? He was such a type of great person, truly a special being. Whenever anyone came to listen to his teachings, for instance, they would become very subdued, quiet and calm.

As he wrote about these thirty-seven practices in order to help us all, we must try to examine these teachings over and over again. We say we are Mahayana practitioners, but if we do not always examine the actual Mahayana practices, this would never do. Therefore we should try to examine ourselves in terms of these thirty-seven practices and see if, in fact, we do accord our actions with them. Amongst them we will find teachings for individuals of the three different levels of motivation, as explained in the "Lam-rim" or "Graded Path".

I shall now give just a short commentary on this text. I have received its lineage from Kunu Lama Rinpoche, Tenzin Gyaltsen, and he received this from the prior Dzogchen Rinpoche in the province of Kham. This is just a little background history and this copy, in fact, I brought with me from Lhasa.

"Obeisance to Lokeshvara"

> "I prostrate always respectfully through the three gateways of my body, speech and mind, to Avalokiteshvara, the Protector (inseparable from), the Supreme Gurus, who, seeing that all phenomena have no true coming or going, makes efforts singly to benefit beings."

The sources for these teachings are from the "Bodhisattvacharyavatara" or "Guide to Bodhisattvas' Way of Life", the "Mahayana Sutralamkara" or "The Adornment of the Mahayana Sutras" and also the "Ratnamala" or "Precious Garland". The text is divided into three sections. The first concerns collecting merit at the beginning, the second the actual teachings and the third is the conclusion. The first of these is divided into two, the initial salutation and the promise to compose. Here we have the first to these two parts, the salutation. The prostration is made to Avalokiteshvara, referred to here as Lokeshvara. As the root of Enlightenment is compassion, and since Avalokiteshvara is its embodiment, the prostration is made to him. Also, to set the seeds and instincts for us to be able to meet with and study Sanskrit in the future, the name of Lokeshvara is given in Sanskrit. The prostration is made to Avalokiteshvara as inseparable from the Gurus and is done with the three gateways of body, speech and mind. The reason for making such prostration is because of the good qualities of such an object of reverence.

What are these good qualities? The root of Mahayana is the Enlightened Motive of Bodhichitta. This is a mind aimed at Enlightenment with the intention to attain it and to do so in order to be able to benefit all living beings. To accomplish these aims we have to practice the six perfections. As a result we are able to attain an Enlightenment that has both a physical and a mental aspect, namely the Form Bodies and Dharmakaya or Wisdom Bodies. To attain these two we need to have accumulated causes that are in a similar category to the results. Thus we need a collection of merit in order to achieve a Form Body of a Buddha and a collection of insight in order to achieve a Buddha's Mind. The basis for these are the two levels of truth.

Lokeshvara is someone who sees that "all phenomena have no true coming or going". When we examine the conventional level of truth, things do in fact come and go. But if we examine the ultimate level, this is not established as being a truly existent or inherently existent coming and going. For example, there is such a thing as cause and effect. Since causes have no inherent existence or are void of true existence, their effects must likewise be void of such existence. Neither has inherent existence, therefore they are established as depending on each other. In other words, the dependently arising nature of all phenomena is established as not being inherently existent. As Nagarjuna has said, things have no true coming, going, abiding and so forth. Thus the phrase "seeing that all phenomena have no true coming or going " refers to Voidness and the fact that the object of prostration here is someone who understands or sees this Voidness with bare perception. Because everything is a dependent arising, because everything dependently arises, everything is void of inherent existence. And because everything is void of inherent existence, things dependently arise by a process of cause and effect.

From delusions as a cause there comes about suffering as a result, and from virtues comes happiness. Since the coming of suffering dependently arises from delusions and non-virtue, and the object of prostration here sees that this is the case with all living beings, his compassion is therefore aimed at them solely for the purpose of helping to show them the way to eliminate their suffering or make it go away. Thus both the wisdom and the method sides are indicated here since we need to have both together without either being missing. From the salutary verse then we can see these two sides. Lokeshvara sees that everything is void of inherent existence and because everything is void he sees that all phenomena arise from cause and effect. Specifically he sees that the suffering of all beings arises or comes from their delusions, and therefore he is compassionately aimed at eliminating that suffering or making it go. Thus the two sides of wisdom and method are praised here with regard to Lokeshvara. Because he sees everything as void, he sees everything as cause and effect. Thus he has compassion for everyone to take them out of their suffering. Do you understand?

The next verse is the promise to compose.

> "Fully Enlightened Buddhas, the sources of benefit and happiness, come from realizing the holy Dharma. Moreover, since this depends on knowing just what are its practices, I shall explain a Bodhisattva's practice."

Buddha first developed Bodhichitta, the Enlightened Motive, in order to benefit everyone. Then once he attained Enlightenment, his single aim has been to benefit all. He tamed his own mind, seeing that he had to eliminate all his own delusions, and that this is the process for everyone to be able to attain happiness. Thus Buddha taught the various methods to do this and we ourselves must practice in the same way as he did. If we practice as he taught then we too shall be able to obtain happiness. Therefore in the text it refers to the Buddhas as "the sources of benefit and happiness".

The Buddha himself was not enlightened from the beginning. He relied on his own Gurus, practiced their teachings and tamed his mind. By the process of eliminating all his delusions he became enlightened. Therefore, he reached his attainment by following or "realizing the holy Dharma."

We should try to understand how we have both a body and a mind. When our eye consciousness sees something, for instance, we do not say that our eye consciousness sees it but that I myself do. If our body becomes sick we say that I am sick. Therefore, the implication of these expressions is either that I am a mind or consciousness or that I am a body. But our body is first formed in our mother's womb and it ends when it decomposes with our death. So "I" cannot be just a body. Maybe then it is the case that I am a mind is dependent on a body. But we respond even to merely seeing a body. The "I", for instance, is not a form, a shape, nor a color. Yet when we see a body in the distance, based on that we say, "Oh, I see my friend" and we become very happy. But that person, if we examine closely, is not just his body. When we go to see a doctor, for instance, the doctor says, "Is your body well?" but obviously we are not just our body. In America in some famous hospitals, we see doctors even prescribing meditation in order to improve people's health. Thus obviously there must be some relationship between the body and mind for them to give that type of non-physical prescription.

But what about this "I" just being the mind? Let us look at the nature of the mind. When we know something, or are clear about or aware of something, we say "I know that thing". But it is very difficult to identify precisely what the mind is. Its definition is just a mere clarity and awareness. It is not something physical that has any color or shape. If we think about it, it is something like a clear space, a very empty space in which all appearances have ceased and in which the awareness of anything can arise or dawn as a mere clarity and awareness within that clear space.

The mind then which arises simultaneously with the winds, drops and so on of the subtle body at the first moment of conception is something that has this nature of mere clarity and awareness. For such a phenomenon to arise it needs, as its immediate cause, something that exists in the same nature or in the same category as it itself. Therefore it is necessary for there to be a prior moment of mere clarity and awareness to act as a cause for the first moment of clarity and awareness at the instant of conception. It is by such lines of reasoning that we can establish or prove the existence of past lifetimes. And if past lives exist it follows that future ones do also.

As this clarity and awareness which we have is something having continuity and which will go on in future lives, it is very important to eliminate the obscurations or films that are over it causing us our various delusions and suffering. In removing them we become able to reach the natural base of consciousness which is just mere clarity and awareness unobscured. This is what can become the Omniscient Mind of a Buddha or an Enlightened Being. Therefore, as the basis in our own mind and in that of Enlightened Being, or in an Omniscient Mind, is the same; the latter type of mind is something we can definitely attain ourselves. A Buddha is not someone who is enlightened from the beginning, he became enlightened by relying on various causes. He abandoned what is necessary to abandon and attained what is necessary to attain. Therefore if we do the same, we can attain the same.

Thus the text says "Fully Enlightened Buddhas, the sources of benefit and happiness, come from realizing the Dharma". How can we ourselves do this? It says, "This depends on knowing just what are its practices". Thus it is not sufficient merely to know about the Dharma. It is necessary to put it into practice and realize it.

I shall leave the text here for today. Have you understood everything? We should practice as much as we can. What we must practice is renunciation, Bodhichitta, and Voidness. We should examine ourselves very carefully and honestly, see what our disposition is, what our own tendencies and inclinations are and then train ourselves in a path that suits us.

Day Two

As I explained yesterday, we are at a special place here where the Buddha became enlightened and many enlightened Beings have been. Nagarjuna and his two spiritual sons, for instance, and many Tibetans as well have stayed in Bodh Gaya. For example, Sangyay Yeshey came here long ago from Kham and became its Abbot. Many others arrived also from all different lands and due to the blessings of this place received many insights. This is a special characteristic of this holy spot. So if we, being here too, have a strong, proper motivation, and if we pray hard, then with much enthusiasm and proper practice we can gain much merit also. Especially for those of you who have come here from Tibet, although the conditions there are so difficult, you should take full advantage of being in such a holy place now to gain much merit. All of us here are very fortunate. At such a time, with such rampant delusions in the world and so much desire and hatred, it is extremely precious to have the opportunity to follow the Buddha's teachings of compassion, love and so on. Although there is so much wealth in the world, there is no way that money can buy freedom from death, old age and other basic problems. Since sufferings comes from the side of the mind, then external circumstances such as wealth cannot eliminate that mental suffering. Thus it is very important to follow religious or spiritual methods, and of all the various traditions it is very wonderful that you have this interest in Buddhism.

Look at the many Westerners who are here among us. They have come because of their sincere interest in Buddhism. They meditate, recite prayers, do practice and know quite a lot. This interest of theirs in Buddhism is due to their having thought about it with logic and reasoning. They have analyzed the teachings of Buddhism in order to accept them. Seeing their example we can see that this is a very precious and important opportunity to be in such a holy place as this, Bodh Gaya. Here we become mindful of all the great acts, deeds and qualities of the Enlightened Beings. As being in such a place so conducive for virtue is really quite rare, we must try to accumulate as much merit as possible. The more we can do, the greater the force will be of our merit because of our being in this special place. Do you understand? While you are here, although selling goods is not forbidden, you should be honest, and although it is all right to receive some profit from your sales, do not be greedy or dishonest. Also, when you circumambulate do not gossip and mentally wander, but be attentive and respectful. And don't throw paper all around on the ground and go to the toilet everywhere. I realize that if you wait in line just to use the toilet you may have to wait for hours, so you have to go elsewhere; be as clean as possible. Tibet is a cold country, whereas here in India at a low elevation the conditions are different. So don't just dirty the place everywhere. Be careful and be responsible.

Also it is very good to do prostration, either bent or outstretched, but do so correctly. Keep your hands flat on the ground and have your palms facing downwards. Offer candles, do things like this. This is very good, it is excellent. Say prayers, meditate and even if it is not with single-minded concentration, it sets very good instincts. The most important thing is to have a very pure motivation. Therefore we must examine our mind and motivation for everything we do. This is very important. We must try to diminish the power of our delusions as much as we can and try to abandon negative activities as much as possible. The best thing to do is to develop an attitude of considering others more important and ourselves as unimportant. This is the essence of the Mahayana. Have a kind and warm heart. Being virtuous in our actions and at heart being kind, warm and loving is the real point. If we engage in external Dharma actions out of pride, competition or jealousy it only leads to a negative karmic debt. Therefore it is important and crucial what we do. We must always examine and correct our motivation. Being here in such a holy, and special place, we must try to have as enlightened a motive as possible. Remaining ever mindful of Buddha's examples of developing Bodhichitta, we should try as much as we can to emulate them. If we develop a kind heart and great motivation in such a place as this, it is very beneficial. Do you understand?

As it says in "Guide to Bodhisattvas' Way of Life", try never to become angry. As is explained there, nothing destroys merit like anger. So try never to lose your temper or become angry with anyone. Try to tame and discipline your mind not to be crude to rough. Instead of being jealous of others' actions, rejoice in the merit of everyone here. Recite the Seven-limbed Puja and think well of all its points. Try to accumulate as much merit as you can. Understand? And if we can accumulate together a little bit here, it will make our lives much better, won't it?

So now set a Bodhichitta motivation to listen to these teachings. It is "The Thirty-Seven Bodhisattva Practices" by Thogmey Zangpo and is divided into three parts; the beginning, the actual discussion and the end. The actual discussion is divided into the three levels of motivation, as explained in the "Lam-rim", the "Graded Path".

> (1) "At this time, when we have obtained a fully endowed human rebirth of liberties and endowments are difficult to find, a Bodhisattva's practice is to listen, think and meditate unwaveringly day and night in order to free ourselves and others from the ocean of cyclic existence."

Dharma is a system of methods to make an unpeaceful mind peaceful and an untamed one tamed. All of us are equal in wanting happiness and not any suffering, and Dharma is what brings this about. But people do not know how to practice it. If we look at our human body, although we might think of it merely in terms of its being in the category or lineage of our parents, if we look more profoundly we see that it is in the category of having liberty and endowments. Liberty means freedom to practice Dharma, and look at us here. We do have the freedom to come here and to practice Dharma, don't we? We are not deaf, we are not missing various faculties that would prevent us from hearing the teachings and so on. We have all the conducive conditions for practice and whatever is non-conducive is not here. We have, in fact, eight liberties and ten endowments.

Many people in the world have a human birth but few have the independence and freedom to practice the Dharma. We are very fortunate therefore to have such a rare opportunity. Also there are spiritual teachers available and present in the world, following the example of the Buddha and carrying on his deeds. These are good effects we are experiencing now have resulted from causes similar to them in the past. In other words, our good fortune now must be from virtuous causes we have previously enacted and therefore to obtain such opportunities and such a working basis once more in the future, we must accumulate the virtuous causes for this now. If we act without attachment, aversion or closed-minded ignorance, it will not be difficult to accumulate virtuous causes for a precious human rebirth in the future. But in fact as we rarely act this way, we must take as much advantage of the present opportunity as we can. Never be discouraged or feel inadequate. We must practice as much virtue as we can.

A virtuous or a tamed mind is not something we can buy in a store, plant in a field or obtain from a bank. It comes from the actual practice of taming our mind. We must practice in order to receive glimpses of insight, lasting realizations and various experiences. Thus we must follow the examples of the great teachers of the past. In Tibet first there were the great Nyingma Lamas, then after there were Atisha and the Kadam lineage, the Sakya Lamas, Marpa, Milarepa and Gampopa of the Kagyu lineage and so on. All of them underwent great difficulties and by exerting tremendous efforts they became enlightened. It is just up to us to follow their example. We should examine ourselves and ask: "What progress have I made in the last five years, the last ten, the last fifteen years in taming my mind?" If we can see that we have indeed made a little improvement then this can encourage us. Do not be proud, or anything like that, but if we realize that over five or ten years we can progress a little then we will not be discouraged over short periods of time.

The actual practice is to hear, think and meditate about the teachings. But when we hear teachings or study them, we should always check our attitude about them. Whatever we hear we should immediately put into practice. We should never have our practice of hearing, thinking and meditating be separate from each other or have any of them missing.

> (2) "A Bodhisattva's practice is to leave our homeland, where desire for our friends shakes us up like water, anger towards enemies burns us like fire, and the closed-minded ignorance of forgetting what is to be adopted and abandoned cloaks us in darkness."

Best is to leave our country, but even if we do not or cannot, we should not have attachment or aversion over it. Do not think, "This is my country, my family," as though there were a findable, inherently existent country for which we could have attachment or hatred of its enemies. Attachment and aversion brings much non-virtue and suffering. These two are the chief of all our delusions and both come from ignorance. But even if we leave our country and go to another, make new friends and then develop attachments and aversions there, this will not do. This is no good. The main point is to abandon attachment and aversion and replace it with an attitude of wishing to help everyone. If there are people to whom we feel attracted and for whom we have attachment, then with just a slight change in their behavior all of a sudden we hate them. But if, instead, we have an attitude of love and compassion to help these persons, then even if they behave badly we will still wish for them to be happy. Thus, we must replace our attachment with an attitude of wishing to help others.

Most of us here have left our country, but there is nothing wonderful or extraordinary about that if we still have attachment and aversion. We must abandon these.

> (3) "A Bodhisattva's practice is to rely on seclusion where, by abandoning negative objects our delusions

> gradually become stymied, by lacking distractions our virtuous practices naturally increase, and by clearing up our awareness, our certainty grows in the Dharma."

If we are away from those who disturb us and we do not have a head full of busy work, then automatically we turn to virtue more easily. Therefore it is most helpful to live in seclusion and quietude. But to be able to meditate in solitude, we need the full force of having heard and thought about the teachings, and this without any attachment or aversion. Thus, we have attained a precious human rebirth and now we must use it properly and not lose this opportunity because it is impermanent. We must turn away then from our obsessive concern with mainly this life, as it says in "The Three Principal Paths". If we put our main emphasis on future lives, then things will go well in this life also. But if all our emphasis is this life, it will not help our future lives at all. Therefore we must turn from being only involved in this life and work to improve our future ones. To do this we must think about impermanence.

> (4) "A Bodhisattva's practice is to give up total concern with this lifetime in which friends and relations a long time together must part their own ways, wealth and possessions gathered with effort must be left behind, and our consciousness, the guest, must depart from our body, its guest house."

If we look at world history, no one in the Three Realms has lived forever. Look at the great places of the past, Nalanda, where great Atisha and others flourished. Now only its ruins are left, but this helps to show us impermanence. Look at the customs and so forth of Tibet of the past. These circumstances are past, they are impermanent and have finished. A hundred years from now it is certain that none of us here will be alive. Our mind-stream of mere awareness and clarity will have gone on; the existence of past and future lifetimes is for certain. But what we experience now will not—our wealth, our prosperity, all of these things which have come from causes in past lifetimes. No matter how close we are with others, our family and so on, we will all have to part and go our own ways. Those who have accumulated virtue will experience happiness; those who haven't, will not. The continuity of the mere "I" labelled on the subtle energy and consciousness goes on for sure, thus we shall experience the fruits of the actions we commit now. Therefore it is crucial what we do.

When we die, we all go alone. Even the Dalai Lama, when he dies, has to go alone. When Mao Tse-tung died, he went alone. Jiang Qing did not accompany him, nor did his masses. All his fame while alive did not help him at all. We can see what happened afterwards. Even such a great man as Mahatma Gandhi went alone. He had to leave his staff, his sandals, his round wire glasses behind. We can see them in his memorial; he has taken nothing along. External material possessions, friends, relatives, nothing helps, not even the body we have received from our parents. As Ghungthang Rinpoche explained, we all have to go alone.

Look at us Tibetans, look at yourselves. Even if we are in such difficult times, we are still human and when we die there is no certainty that we will be human again. If we do not make some progress now while we are human, what can we do later in another lifetime not as a human. Now, of course, we have to eat. Except for great beings who live on single-minded concentration, all of us have to eat solid meals. So obviously we have to plant food and do things for this lifetime. But we should not have this to be our total obsession. We should devote maybe 30% of our time to this lifetime and 70% to the future, or better 50\50. But the main point is not to be totally involved with this life alone.

> (5) "A Bodhisattva's practice is to abandon bad friends with whom, when we associate, our three poisonous attitudes increase, our actions of listening, thinking and meditating decrease and our love and compassion turn to nil."

We must think then mostly of our future lives and to do so we need friends. They are important because they influence us very much. Even if our own hearing and thinking of teachings is quite meagre their good example can influence us to do more. It is important then to have friends of the same disposition as ourselves. Why? Because as it says in the verse, bad friends or misleading ones can harm us by their company, therefore we must abandon them. But of course this means that we should still have love for them; just stay out of their influence.

> (6) "A Bodhisattva's practice is to cherish more than our own body, our holy spiritual teachers, by devoting ourselves to whom our faults become eliminated and our good qualities come to increase like the waxing moon."

If we have positive-minded friends and keep the good company of Gurus or Spiritual Teachers, they exert the best influence on us. Of course we need a Guru who suits us, but even if such a person is pleasing to our mind, he must be fully qualified. We Tibetans have Tulkus or Incarnate Lamas with famous names, but they must be fully qualified, otherwise it is meaningless. Therefore we should put aside the person's title as a Tulku and check his own personal qualifications. If he is fully qualified then he is a Guru or a Lama. But many Tulkus in fact are not Lamas. They have no qualifications, even though they might have a very large estate and a great deal of wealth. Money, a big name and fame, however, do not make someone a Lama. Therefore we must check their actual qualifications, their studies and so forth. Such careful scrutiny is extremely important. Buddha emphasized it, as did Je Tsong-Khapa. Guru-devotion between disciples and their Spiritual Teachers is extremely crucial. If the Guru is fully qualified then we can fully entrust ourselves to him and do whatever he says, as was the case with Naropa and Tilopa. If Tilopa told him to jump, Naropa did so without hesitation. But if he is not such a person, we should not just do anything that just anyone tells us. We do not go out and jumps off this stupa monument simply because some fool tells us to do that, do we?

The main point is for us beginners to have a firm basis or foundation in moral discipline upon which we can build. The way we Tibetans practice is very good. We have a basis of morality, on top of which we have the Mahayana practice of love and compassion. Then at the peak we have the practice of tantra, and this is of all four of its classes. In fact, we Tibetans are the only Buddhists who practice the entire path of the Buddha's teachings and this on the basis of one person practicing it all. In Thailand, Burma and Sri Lanka, for instance, they have only the discipline part and lack the Mahayana as well as the tantras. In Japan, Korea and some other places where there is Mahayana, they have the tantras but only the first three classes: kriya, charya and yoga. They have nothing of anuttarayoga tantra, and fourth class. Some places have a view of Voidness but only that of the Chittamatra or of the Yogacharya Svatantrika systems and not the Prasangika view. Some places seem to have Mahayana with no basis of discipline and others even try to have Tantrayana with both of the other two missing. It is only among the Tibetans that we have the full, entire path and practice incorporated into one person, and this person should be each of us ourselves.

> (7) "A Bodhisattva's practice is to take refuge in the Precious Gems by seeking protection from whom we are never deceived—since who can worldly gods

protect, when they themselves are still bound in the prison of cyclic existence."

This brings us to refuge, and when we do so we must be mindful of the good qualities of the Three Jewels of Refuge. The word for Buddha in Tibetan is "Sangyay". "Sang" means to eliminate everything that is to be abandoned, to eliminate all faults, and "gyay" means to realize and achieve all good qualities. The Sanskrit word "Dharma" means to hold, to hold one back from what is non-conducive. In other words, following the Dharma holds us back from suffering. Actually, the Dharma Refuge refers to the Noble Truths of Cessation and the Path. The cessation of the fleeting taints over our mind, their dissolution into the pure sphere of Voidness, is a true cessation. The path-like minds that have bare perception of Voidness are true paths. These two are the Dharma Refuge. The Sangha Refuge refers to Aryas or Noble Ones, those who have such bare perception of Voidness. Thus these are the Three Jewels of Refuge. Buddha is like a doctor, Dharma is like medicine, or more precisely, the path of the cure and the state of being cured are like the Noble Truths of the Path and Cessation, and the Sangha are like nurses to help.

We all dislike suffering, from the slightest discomfort upwards, and we wish liberation from it. Its state of elimination and the methods to eliminate it are like the Dharma Refuge. We need a teacher of this process and this is the Buddha Refuge, and friends to help, which is the Sangha Refuge. Furthermore, we need to be confident in the refuge objects' ability to give us protection, plus we need to have fear or dread of suffering and the desire for relief. These act as the causes for taking refuge. As Buddha taught a way to eliminate the cause of suffering such that its cessation will come about, he is worthy of being an object of refuge. We have met with the teachings of such a Buddha and thus we must take refuge. We have a resultant refuge which we can take in our future attainment of the cessation of suffering and Enlightenment, and a causal refuge in the Three Jewels now to bring us to this state. Therefore all of you please take refuge.

Day Three

Look at all the people around you, whether they are close or distant, rich or poor, all of us are equal in wanting happiness and no suffering. The best way to accomplish this is the practice of Dharma. We have a fully endowed human body and have met with the complete teachings of discipline, Mahayana and tantra and have likewise met with well-qualified Gurus. Therefore we must set a full Mahayana motivation to eliminate all our delusions, attain all good qualities and reach Enlightenment. The basic point is to develop a warm and kind heart. This is the root of all happiness for ourselves and others, both superficially and ultimately. It is the root of Bodhichitta which brings us Enlightenment and thus the ability to bring happiness to everyone. Therefore as much as we can we should develop a kind heart. Do not just say words like "May I develop a kind heart." What we have to do is actually train and practise in the stages to attain it. We must know the methods and then put them into practice. The full teachings are found in the 100 volumes of the Kangyur and the 200 of the Tengyur commentaries by the Indian masters. The main Lama who brought the full Lam-rim stages of training the mind to Tibet was Atisha, and his "Budhipathapradita", or "Lamp for the Path to Enlightenment", is the root source of this text, "The Thirty-Seven Bodhisattva Practices". As it is short and easy to understand, we should try to memorise and then often recite it, thinking of the meaning, and put it into practice.

Now listen to the continuation of the teachings on this text. First we must recognise the precious human body and think to take advantage of it. As it is certain that we will die and lose it, we must turn from our obsession with this life and eventually turn from that with future lives as well. To do so we should initially think about death and impermanence and that when we die we can be reborn in one of the three lower realms. We cannot see the hell beings or hungry ghosts, but we know about the animals and their sufferings. We see how they are abused, beaten, exploited for their labour, used cruelly in medical experiments, sacrificed for their meat, and so forth. In Buddhism we must develop kindness for them. In other religions they feel killing animals is not much different from chopping down a tree, or picking a vegetable but in Buddhism it is different. We actually look at and take their suffering seriously and consider how we could easily be reborn as one of them.

The person who teaches the path of how to avoid being reborn as an animal is the Fully Enlightened Buddha. He taught the path of cause and effect, of what actions are to be abandoned and which are to be practiced . We should try to learn as much as we can of the Buddha's perfect teachings, for they are without any faults and they offer a total refuge. As we were saying yesterday, the Buddha, Dharma and Sangha are the Three Jewels of Refuge. Only these three offer a never-failing refuge and protection. Although there is no fault in going to worldly gods for help as friends, it is improper to seek our ultimate refuge in them.

Look at the monks in the monasteries of Thailand and Burma; they are really excellent. In their temples they have only representations of the Buddha Sakyamuni and no one else. In Tibetan temples we may have a picture of Buddha Sakyamuni but also there are various exotic-looking protectors and so forth. In Japan there are pictures of just the main teachers and almost no representations of Sakyamuni Buddha. Of course there is the fact of the Buddha's being inseperable from the Gurus and appearing in many forms, but this is something different. The point is that the main one to whom we should turn for blessings and virtuous conduct is the Buddha Sakyamuni. Often people criticise us and say that we Tibetans forget about the Buddha and just beat drums before pictures of proctectors. There is much danger in this, so be careful. But enough on this point.

Concerning the Sangha Refuge, the practice in Thailand and Burma also is excellent. The monks are treated with great respect and are supported by the householders and given alms. This is excellent. Often people feel that there are actually only two Jewels of Refuge, the Buddha and the Dharma, and that the Sangha is unnecessary. We can forget about them. There is no need for everyone to be monks and nuns, but we should check our own disposition, and if it suits us, being ordained is best. But at least never criticize monks and nuns. We should examine and criticize only ourselves. The Sangha is very important for setting examples and for symbolizing the Buddha's teachings. We must be very careful about our own karma and about what we say and do.

> (8) "A Bodhisattva's practice is never to commit any negative actions even at the cost of our life, because the Sage Buddha has said that the extremely difficult to endure sufferings of the unfortunate rebirths are the result of negative actions."

In short, if we do good, good comes from it.and if we do bad, bad comes from it. It is very simple. The effect follows in the same category as the cause. It never fails and moreover, from small causes we can experience extensive results. In countries as well, any horrible conditions that happen come from past karmic debts due to negative actions. In Tibet for instance, we sometimes have drought, our crops fail, sometimes there are wars, invasions and so forth. All of these are due to our lack of merit and past negative actions. If we do not have any merit then no matter what we do it will not bring about good conditions. Therefore we should always wish for others' happiness. Like concerning the Chinese, we can only wish them well. We should not wish that bad things befall them. What they experience will be the results of their own actions.

Negative behavior comes from our delusions and from these we collect black karmic debts which bring us nothing but suffering. Negative actions can be of body, speech or mind. An example for one of the body would be, for instance, killing, which is taking the life of anything from a human down to an insect. It is very bad to kill, so we should restrain ourselves as much as we can. All beings have an equal right to life and cherish their life as much as we do. If we prick our finger with a thorn, we say "Ouch, I hurt". Everybody feels exactly the same, all beings. It is especially terrible to sacrifice animals; they do that in some lands. In the past they did this in Kinnaur, Spiti and some places in Nepal, and even in certain districts in Tibet. Superficially the people there take refuge in me, the Dalai Lama, and then sacrifice animals. This is very bad. Saying the mantra of compassion "Om mani padme hum" and yet sacrificing, that will never, never do.

Next is stealing. This also is very negative. Sexual misconduct is to have relations with another person's spouse, or with someone who has a relation with someone else, and not seeing anything wrong in so doing. When we look at the historical literature, most of the various discords and fights in royal families came from sexual misconduct. It is very destructive. Next is lying. This too is extremely negative. Of course to lie to protect someone's life is something else, but we should always be honest. If we lie, it brings only unhappiness. We sit in fear that somebody is going to find us out. That always makes for a very uneasy mind, doesn't it? Next is divisive language, causing others to be unfriendly and apart. We hear bad things about someone and then spread it; this is very destructive. We must try to bring other people together. When people live and work together, their harmony is based on their mutual confidence. When we look at the Chinese, for instance, they speak of everybody as being comrades, but this is only at the discussion table. Outside they will not even share a bar of soap with each other. This is because they have no confidence, they do not trust one another. And this comes from causing divisiveness among others. Therefore never use divisive language.

Next is abusive language, calling other people bad names like "beggar" and so forth. It hurts them, it does not bring happiness at all. Gossip is chattering always meaningless things; it is a complete waste of time. Then there is covetous thought. Someone else has something nice which we would like, and we walk along directing all our attention at this object and wishing only to have it. If we are not careful we will walk right into a wall! Ill-will is next. This is also very bad. It just makes us unhappy. It usually does not hurt the other person, it hurts only ourselves. It is very self-destructive to hold grudges and to wish others ill. We can never solve problems by holding a grudge. Problems can only be solved through compassion, love and patience so never harbor ill-will. Next is distorted views; denying what exists or making up something which does not.

These ten then, from killing to holding distorted views, are the ten negative actions. We should realize their disadvantages and refrain from them. The actual practice then is, from seeing their drawbacks, to refrain ourselves, with enthusiasm and conscious effort, from killing, lying and so forth. Even if we cannot refrain completely we should try to lessen them as much as we can. This is what follows from taking refuge.

Now comes the teaching for a person on the intermediate level of motivation.

> (9) "A Bodhisattva's practice is to work with keen interest for the supreme, never-changing state of Liberation, as the pleasures of the Three Realms are

phenomena that perish in a moment, all at once,
like dew on the tips of grass."

No matter where we are born in the Three Realms, it is like merely being on different floors of a burning building. Everywhere is suffering, so we must by all means attain liberation from it. Samsara, or cyclic existence, refers to the suffering contaminated aggregates that we receive from karma and delusions. We should think about this. Although we have a precious human rebirth, yet if we are under the power of karma and delusions and have no independence, we can only create more suffering. Therefore, we must try to free ourselves from these repeating syndromes. Whatever wordly pleasures we have are not ultimate. They are merely superficial and only temporary. We can fall to a lower rebirth at any time.

If our suffering comes from our very own aggregates physical and mental faculties, which are under the power of karma and delusions, then where can we run from our contaminated aggregates? Think about that. If our own aggregates themselves are in the nature of suffering, how can we escape them? The source of suffering is our delusions, the main ones of which are attachment and aversion. These both come from ignorance, the ignorance of grasping for inherent existence but this is a distorted view. On the other hand, by cultivating the opponent for this, namely the opposite view, that inherent existence does not exist, and by accustoming ourselves to it, then the more familiar we are with it, the less will be our ignorance. The stains of ignorance over the mind are fleeting; they can be removed. The ignorance of grasping for inherent existence and the understanding of the lack of inherent existence are both aimed at the same object. Thus when we have one we cannot have the other at the same time. It is in this way that the discriminating awareness or wisdom of Voidness acts as the opponent to ignorance. With this wisdom we eliminate attachment and aversion and thus gain liberation from suffering.

Some people say that attachment and aversion or hostility are the nature of the mind, and that it is almost as if a person is not alive, if he does not have such feelings. But if these were the nature of the mind, then just as is the case when we accept mere awareness and clarity as its nature, these feelings of attachment and hostility should be present all the time. But we see that anger can be quelled, it does not last forever. Thus it is a mistaken view to feel that it is a natural part of life and the nature of the mind to have attachment and aversion.

We need discriminating awareness or wisdom then to see the two levels of truth, that ultimately all is void of inherent existence, yet on a conventional level dependent arising is never false. This is the training in higher wisdom and for it we need the training in high concentration as its base in order not to have any mental wandering and so forth. For this we need the training in higher discipline, either as an ordained person or even as a householder. For instance there are the householder vows, the five lay vows, and it is important at least to keep these. Thus we need the practice of the three higher training.

Next are the teachings for a person on the advanced level of motivation.

> (10) "A Bodhisattva's practice is to develop an Enlightened Motive of Bodhichitta in order to liberate limitless sentient beings because if our mothers, who have been kind to us from beginningless time, are suffering, what can we do with just our own happiness."

All sentient beings, as widespread as space, wish for happiness and no suffering, the same as we do. They are so numerous and if we ignore them and think only of our purpose, it is pathetic, not to mention unfair. We should place ourselves on one side and all other beings on the other. We all wish happiness and not suffering; the only difference is that we are one and they are numberless. So who could see it as fair or reasonable to favour one over everybody else? Bodhisattvas work and wish only for other people's happiness. There is no need to mention that of course they achieve Enlightenment, but besides that, while on the path they do not become unhappy. The harder they work for others and the more they ignore themselves, the happier they become, which then encourages them to work even harder. But if we work only for our own purposes and ignore others, all we obtain is unhappiness, dissatisfaction and discouragement. It is funny it is like that. So we must try to lessen our selfishness and increase our concern for others as much as we can and by so doing we will find that, on the side, we will be a happier person.

If we are working only for the purpose of others then, as is described in "Guide to Bodhisattvas' Way of Life", we will never be afraid where or in what conditions we might be reborn. Wherever we find ourselves, we will work there for the sake of helping others. The same is emphasized in "The Precious Garland" by Nagarjuna. To work only for the sake of others and ignore our own purposes is the way to attain Buddhahood. We say we are Mahayanists, but as Je Tsong-Khapa has said, we must have a Mahayana personality in order to be considered a Mahayanist. Therefore we must work for the sake of others. If we look around for ways to be helpful and if we develop an Enlightened Motive of Bodhichitta, then automatically things will work out to benefit everyone. So as much as we can we should follow the Mahayana training and practice. Do you understand?

Now what is a Bodhisattva? Similar to what was explained about the word "Buddha", the first syllable of the Tibetan for "Bodhi" is "Jhang" which means to eliminate faults, while the second, "chub", means to attain all good qualities. Actually there are two "Bodhis" or states of Perfection and what is being referred to here is not the lesser one of the Arhats but the higher one of a Buddha's Enlightenment. "Sattva" means one who has his mind aimed at this attainment of Bodhi or Perfection, to benefit all. Thus we need two aims together. We need to be aimed at sentient beings in order to benefit them and to be aimed at Enlightenment to be able to do that. That is Bodhichitta and this is what we must develop. How do we do that?

> (11) "A Bodhisattva's practice is to purely exchange our own happiness for the suffering of others because all our sufferings come from desiring our own happiness, while a fully Enlightened Buddha is born from the attitude of wishing others well."

How does all suffering come from wishing only our own happiness? Such a self-centered wish leads us to commit much non-virtue in order to accomplish our selfish aims and as a result we experience suffering. Buddhahood, on the other hand, comes from helping others. Therefore we have to exchange our attitude and instead of wishing for our own happiness and ignoring others' suffering, we should wish only for others' happiness and ignore ourselves. To do this we train in the practice known as "taking and giving," namely taking on others' suffering and giving them our happiness. To help us do this there is a very good and useful visualization. We should visualize ourselves in our ordinary form on the right, selfish and wishing only our own happiness. On the left visualize infinite, numberless living beings all wanting happiness. Then we should stand back in our mind as a witness and judge: "Which is more important, this selfish person here or all the others?" Think which side we would favour and which would we want to join, the side of the selfish person or that of all these pathetic beings, who equally deserve happiness? Such practice like this and others mentioned in "Guide to Bodhisattvas' Way of Life" are very beneficial.

(12) "A Bodhisattva's practice is, even if someone under the power of great desire steals or causes others to steal all our wealth, to dedicate to him our body, wealth and virtues of the three times."

Now we have developed Bodhicitta. But to attain Enlightenment we must engage in the Bodhisattva actions. If someone steals from us there is the danger of becoming angry. But if we are practicing to attain Enlightenment and are giving away everything to others, then this so-called thief already owns our former possessions. He has taken them now because in fact they already are his. Thus we should dedicate to him not only these possessions that he has taken, or which we think he has stolen from us, but even further our body and virtues of the three times.

(13) "A Bodhisattva's practice is, even if while we have not the slightest fault ourselves, or if someone were to chop off our heads, to accept on ourselves these black karmic debts with the power of compassion."

If others harm us we must have compassion towards them and accept on ourselves all these harms of others.

(14) "A Bodhisattva's practice, is, even if someone were to publicize throughout the billion worlds all sorts of unpleasant things about us, to speak in return about their good qualities with an attitude of love."

When others abuse or say bad things about us, we must never return it. Never say nasty things back, but only speak kindly of them, as it says in "Guide to Bodhisattvas' Way of Life".

(15) "A Bodhisattva's practice is, even if someone exposes our faults or says foul words about us in the

> midst of a crowd of many beings, to bow to him respectfully, recognizing him as our teacher."

Even if others humiliate or embarrass us in front of others, we should act as taught in the training of the mind. If others disgrace us or point out our faults, they are in fact our teachers. Thus we should thank them for making us aware of our shortcomings and show them great respect.

> (16) "A Bodhisattva's practice is, even if someone whom we have raised and cherished like our own child, were to regard us as his enemy, to have special loving kindness for him like a mother towards her child stricken with an illness."

If a child is naughty when he is ill, no matter how bad he is, his mother would still love him. This is the way we should view all beings.

> (17) "A Bodhisattva's practice is, even if someone our equal or inferior were to try to demean us out of the power of his pride, to receive him on the crown of our head respectively, like a Guru."

The same is true when others try to compete with us. We must develop patience. As it says in "Guide to Bodhisattvas' Way of Life", if we had no enemies we could not develop patience. Thus we need someone annoying towards whom to develop a tolerant attitude. We cannot develop patience with our mind aimed at our Guru or at a Buddha. We need an enemy at whom to aim it. For instance, I think about myself. If someone writes in the newspaper or calls the Dalai Lama a weak refugee and so on, if I am practicing sincerely I try to develop patience with him. Since we need a teacher to help train us in patience, an enemy or someone who hates us is very important as this teacher. If we think more about it, enemies are extremely important, aren't they? If we are practicing

Mahayana we must cultivate patience and endure difficult situations, but how can we really practice Mahayana without enemies? In short, to exchange our attitudes concerning self and others we need many trials and tribulations, many trying situations. Therefore enemies or people who are very annoying and difficult are extremely important and precious.

> (18) "A Bodhisattva's practice is, even if we are destitute in our livelihood and always abused by people, sick with terrible diseases or afflicted by ghosts, to accept on ourselves the sufferings of all beings and not be discouraged."

There are two very difficult situations for Dharma practice. One is when, due to past causes, we are in very difficult straits, poor and so on. Then we become discouraged. The other is if we are extremely comfortable and rich and then we become prideful and arrogant. We must be careful in both cases. If we are very sick, for instance, then if we practice exchanging self with others and also taking and giving, we will become very happy that we are sick. In fact, we will wish to take on the sickness and suffering of others.

> (19) "A Bodhisattva's practice is, even if we are sweetly praised, bowed to with their heads by many beings, or have obtained riches like those of the children of the Lord of Wealth, never to be conceited by seeing that worldly prosperity has no essence."

This is the other extreme, the other crucial situations. If we are very well-esteemed and everything goes well for us, we can become very prideful about that, lazy and arrogant. As this blocks our practice, we must see that such worldly good fortune has no essence at all.

> (20) "A Bodhisattva's practice is to tame our own mindstream with the martial arts of love and com-

> passion because, if we do not subdue the enemy which is our own hostility, then even if we have subdued an external enemy, more will come."

There is no enemy worse than anger. If we look at the world, like for instance the situation of World War II, we can see that it all came about because of anger and hatred. At that time the Western nations and Russia were allies and even though they won the war that did not conquer their own hostility! As they are now still left with this poison, we find the Soviet Union pitted against the West as enemies. If war comes again in the future, it will occur once more because of anger and hatred. But if we wish peace and happiness, this can never come about without the elimination of these negative attitudes. Peace and happiness will come only if we develop love and compassion. Therefore we must train in the martial art of love to overcome hatred.

> (21) "A Bodhisattva's practice is immediately to abandon whatever objects cause our attachment and desires to increase, for objects of our desire are like salt water, the more we indulge in them our thirst for them increase in turn."

No matter what we are attracted to we are never satisfied with it, we never have enough. It is like drinking salt water, we are never quenched as is described in "The Precious Garland". Think of an example, for instance, like when we have a rash. If we scratch it, it feels nice, but if we are attached to that nice feeling, then the more we scratch, it just makes it worse. It gets sore, it starts to bleed, becomes infected and is a mess. The best thing is to cure the rash from its base so that we will have no desire to scratch it at all.

> (22) "A Bodhisattva's practice is not to apply ourselves mentally to any signs of takers of objects and

> objects taken, by realizing that however things appear, they are from our own mind and that the nature of mind is, from the beginning, free of extremes of fabricated modes of existence."

This seems to be Svatantrika vocabulary, but that is not necessarily so. When it says here that these appearances are "from our own mind," this means that they are the play of our mind in the sense that the karma accumulated through our mind brings about all appearances. The mind itself, from the beginning, is free of extremes of inherent existence. If we understand this, then we will not apply our mind to considering that this is the consciousness that understands Voidness and that is the object of this consciousness, namely Voidness. Rather we will simply place our mind in meditative equipoise on the pure, non-affirming negation which is Voidness. This is the practice that is outlined here.

> (23) "A Bodhisattva's practice is to abandon attachment and desire through, when we meet with a pleasing object, not regarding it as truly existent even though it appears beautifully, like a summer's rainbow."

Although things appear beautifully like a rainbow, we should see that they are void of inherent existence and not be attached.

> (24) "A Bodhisattva's practice is, at the time when meeting with adverse conditions, to see them as deceptive, for various types of suffering are like the death of our child in a dream, and to take such deceptive appearances to be true as a tiresome waste."

Thus, we should see everything as deceptive appearances and not be depressed by difficult conditions.

These are the teachings on developing Bodhichitta. Next is the practice of the perfections.

> (25) "A Bodhisattva's practice is to give generously without hope for anything in return or something to ripen because, if those who would wish Enlightenment must give away even their body, what need to mention our own external possessions."

This is the practice of generosity.

> (26) "A Bodhisattva's practice is to safeguard morality without worldly intents because, if we cannot fulfil our own aims without moral discipline, to wish to fulfil the aims of others is a joke."

Most important is to have moral discipline, especially the discipline of refraining from negative actions. Without it, how can we help anyone?

> (27) "A Bodhisattva's practice is to meditate on patience, without anger or resentment for anyone because, for a Bodhisattva wishing to make use of virtue, all those who do harm are the same as treasures of great gems."

We need much patience. For a Bodhisattva wishing to create the merit to be able to attain Enlightenment, those who do harm, our enemies, are as precious as gems because with them we can practice patience. This brings about a collection of merit which will bring about our Enlightenment.

> (28) "A Bodhisattva's practice is to exert joyous effort, the source of good qualities for the sake of all beings, as we see the effort of Shravakas and Pratyekabuddhas who, in working only for their own sake, are not swayed even if their heads were to be in flames."

This refers to exerting enthusiastic perseverance with joyous effort. If the Hinayana practitioners can work so hard to attain their goal for themselves, then we as Mahayanists working for the sake of all must work even harder.

> (29) "A Bodhisattva's practice is to meditate on meditative concentration which surpasses the four formless absorptions, by realizing that penetrative insight possessing perfect mental quiescence can destroy the delusions completely."

This refers to the perfection of meditative concentration and here in the sutra context. Thus in order to be able to realize penetrative insight or "vipashyana", we need to have beforehand mental quiescence, or "samatha", to hold it. Then we will have inseparable mental quiescence and penetrative insight.

> (30) "A Bodhisattva's practice is to meditate on wisdom which possesses methods and has no conceptions about the inherent existence of the three spheres, because without wisdom the five perfections cannot bring us complete Enlightenment."

We cannot attain Enlightenment with only the method side, namely the first five perfection alone. We need the wisdom aspect as well. Thus we must cultivate inseparable method and wisdom with which we see that the three spheres of any virtuous action of these perfection, namely the action, the actor and the act itself, and all avoid of inherent existence.

Next concerns the Bodhisattvas' daily practice.

> (31) "A Bodhisattva's practice is continually to examine our own mistakes and abandon them because, if we do not examine our own mistakes ourselves, it is possible that with a Dharmic external form we can commit something non-Dharmic."

In other words, we must always check our own delusions each day, because as it says here it is quite possible externally to appear to be proper but in fact not to be proper at all.

> (32) "A Bodhisattva's practice is not to say that any person who has entered the Mahayana Great Vehicle has any faults because, if under the power of delusions we find fault with someone else who is a Bodhisattva, we ourselves will get the worst,"

We should never look at others with the idea of trying to pick or find faults in them. We never know who others might be or what their attainment is. Especially as a Mahayana practitioner we should only have thoughts of helping and benefiting others, not faulting them.

> (33) "A Bodhisattva's practice is to abandon attachment to homes of relatives and friends and homes of patrons because, under the power of wanting gain and respect, we will fight with each other and our activities of hearing, thinking and meditating will decline."

There is much danger if we always stay in the homes of patrons, relatives and so forth. We inevitably become entangled in very complicated situations of arguments, disputes and so on. Therefore we should avoid attachment to such places.

> (34) "A Bodhisattva's practice is to abandon harsh language displeasing to the minds of others because harsh words disturb others' minds, and cause our ways of Bodhisattva behavior to decline."

The root of anger is attachment to our own side. But here the anger itself is stressed especially when it leads to abusive language. Such harsh sounding words destroy our merit, disturb others and cause great harm.

> (35) "A Bodhisattva's practice is to have the soldiers of mindfulness and alertness holds the opponent's weapons and forcefully to destroy delusions like

> attachment and so forth as soon as they first arise because, when we are habituated to delusions, it is difficult for opponents to reverse them."

As soon as attachment or aversion arises, we should immediately employ mindfulness and awareness to oppose them.

> (36) "In short, a Bodhisattva's practice is to work for others' purposes by continually possessing mindfulness and alertness to know, no matter what our activity, how we are acting and further what the condition is of our minds."

As it says in "Guide to Bodhisattvas' Way of Life" we must continually examine our mind and see its condition. Then with mindfulness we should immediately apply the various opponents to any delusions. For instance, if we were on a caravan and reached the northern Plateau of Tibet, we would be very mindful not to go just anywhere but would choose the correct path very carefully. In the same way, we should not allow our mind to go just anywhere.

> (37) "A Bodhisattva's practice is, with the wisdom that purifies the three spheres, to dedicate for Enlightenment, in order to eliminate the suffering of limitless beings, the virtue realized by these efforts,"

Thus, the last Bodhisattva practice mentioned here is to dedicate the merit of all these actions. This completes the actual body of the text and next is the third part of the outline, the conclusion.

> "Having followed the words of the holy beings and the meaning of what has been spoken in the sutras, tantras and treatises, I have arranged these Thirty-Seven Bodhisattva practices for those who wish to train in the Bodhisattvas' path."

The author has taken these teachings from various sources and condensed them into these thirty-seven practices.

> "Because my intelligence is feeble and my learning small, I may not have written this in a poetic fashion that would please the erudite. But because I have relied on the sutras and the words of the holy ones, I believe these are unmistakenly a Bodhisattva's practice."

Next the author apologizes if he has committed any faults.

> "But since it is difficult for someone dull-witted like myself to fathom the depth and extent of the great waves of a Bodhisattva's actions, I request the holy ones to be patient with my mass of faults such as contradictions and unconnected lines."

Then he ends with the dedication.

> "By the virtue from this may all beings never abide in the extremes, of Samsara and Nirvana but with supreme, ultimate and conventional Bodhichitta, become equals of the Protector Avalokiteshvara."

This concludes "Thirty-Seven Bodhisattva Practices" by Thogmey Zangpo.

Day Four

As we are all here in a special place, we must set a special attitude or motivation, and that of Bodhicitta, to attain Enlightenment for the sake of all beings. This should be completely sincere. Buddha himself attained his Enlightenment by the power of his pure Bodhichitta motivation. All this qualities and attainments were dependent on that Enlightened Motive, so we should pray to develop such a mind ourselves as much as possible and have it ever increase.

These last days we have accumulated some merit through these teachings. Let us now continue today with "The Three Principal Paths" by Je Tsong-Khapa. These three refer to renunciation, Bodhichitta and a correct view of Voidness.

Renunciation is based on the attitude with which we turn our minds completely away from all wishes for cyclic existence. Our attainment of Liberation is dependent on having such a renunciation. Bodhichitta is the attitude or intention to attain Enlightenment to benefit all living beings. The correct view of Voidness is seeing the actual abiding nature of reality. Concerning this view, or understanding of Voidness, of reality, of non inherent existence, if it is held by a mind of renunciation it brings Liberation. This is done by eliminating the obstacles that prevent Liberation, namely the delusions which keep us in cyclic existence or samsara. If this understanding of the correct view of Voidness is held by a mind of Bodhichitta, it eliminates as well the obstacles preventing Omniscience, namely the instincts of grasping for true existence, and thereby we attain Enlightenment. Therefore a correct view of Voidness is the main opponent that destroys the obstacles, and it is assisted by either renunciation, or both renunciation and Bodhichitta.

The Hinayana teachings entail renunciation and the correct view of Voidness in order to reach their goal. The Mahayana adds to these Bodhichitta to eliminate all obstacles completely. Thus the three principal aspects of the path, renunciation, Bodhichitta and Voidness, incorporate the essence of all the Hinayana and Mahayana teachings.

Our famous tantras, which have the profound subject of the subtle bodies, winds, energy-channels and drops, have as their foundation these same three principal paths – renunciation, an extremely strong Bodhichitta motivation and a full understanding of Voidness as taught by Nagarjuna and his two spiritual sons. Then in addition to these, we set our pride or dignity on the potential of what we can achieve from the subtle minds and consciousness. In this way we hold the dignity of either a Form Body or a Dharma Wisdom Body of a Buddha, or on, both of these. Although we do not actually have these bodies at the time of practice, yet based on our strong Bodhichitta motivation to attain this Enlightened State of benefit for all living beings, we gradually become able to achieve them through these practices of maintaining the dignity of these Bodies.

Thus the three principal aspects are the basis of the entire sutra and tantra paths. In any case, we must always try to follow a combined practice of wisdom and methods, trying to help others, collecting merit and so forth.

This particular text is quite short, only a few verses. I first studied it myself with Tagtra Rinpoche and later with many others, including Trijang Dorjechang. We should set a proper motivation to listen to these teachings. If we set a kind heart as our motivation, this is the source of all happiness. But if we lack such a heart, and instead are proud, pretentious and so on, this only brings unhappiness and uneasiness. The effects in future lives of whether we will be either a cultivated, gentle person or a rough, crude being will be seen in terms of our conduct in this life. Even if we do not accept the existence of future lives, yet having a kind heart, or on the other hand being coarse and crude, will bring either happiness or unhappiness in turn now.

The most important is our daily conduct. Even if there were no such thing as future lives, there is no harm in being gentle, it helps in our daily life. If there are future lives, then even more so will we benefit from being a gentle, kind person. So be friendly, kind to each other, and not just in theory. We must do so in terms of actual people and actual situations we encounter in our daily life. This is the essence of the Dharma and it is not difficult to follow. It is not something we go and buy in a store, but rather it is something that we practice ourselves.

Look at the Chinese, for instance. They are proper objects for our compassion. They do not know what is right and wrong, they do not know the consequences of their acts, so we should show them compassion. You yourselves, we should all try to be kind and refined. Look at drinkers of chang (beer), and of alcohol--this is a very bad custom. They become drunk, raucous, crude, rude and cause much disturbance. Buddha said that as a consequence of drinking we very often will commit many non-virtues of body, speech and mind. Therefore it is not good at all to drink. The same is true with smoking. Although it is not forbidden and the disadvantages of it are not mentioned specifically in Buddha's teachings, yet as we see from what Western doctors say, it is extremely dangerous for our health. If there were some particular purpose in smoking, that would be all right. But if there is none, as is mostly the case, then it is best not to. The same as with taking snuff and so on, it is not to use these things at all. In such ways, by abandoning these crude types of habits, we will become more and more of a gentle person, a cultivated and refined person. The more we can do this the better. If we see other gentlemen and gentlewomen, we should rejoice in their examples and try to become as gentle and cultivated as we can ourselves. Do you understand? Be more and more mindful to be gentle, cultivated, loving and to have a warm heart. Look at the disadvantages of being crude, raucous, selfish and rough. We must always remind ourselves of them. If we have a kind heart, this brings happiness, good fortune, health and peace of mind. This helps me a lot in my own thinking. We are all the same, we all want happiness, so we should all do the same, be gentle and kind.

Look at those who are coming here from Tibet. They do not harp on all the difficulties they have had in these last twenty odd years and say how pathetic we are, and feel sorry for themselves. Rather they come here being very interested in the Dharma. We Tibetans who have been living here also should not harbor grudges against the Chinese. We should feel how fortunate we are to have had the opportunity to be in India and practice the Dharma. I know many others who have been oppressed by the Chinese and were held prisoners there, and without Buddhist training they went mad with their hatred and anger. So it is most important not to be angry like that, but to be cultivated and try to nurture a kind heart. It makes a huge difference at the time of our death. Look at Hitler. Although he was so powerful during his life, his hatred overcame him and when he died he was so desperate and unhappy he took poison and killed himself. Stalin likewise died in a state of great fear and Mao Tse-tung passed away in very difficult straits. Therefore, it is important to be kind and have a warm heart in our entire life so that when we die, we can do so with peace of mind.

In all the countries I have been travelling, I teach exactly the same point. Whether I am in the West, or even when I was in the Soviet Union, I told them all to have a kind heat, be friendly towards everyone in a non-partisan fashion and be equally loving to all . Whenever I go to various places, I see people of many different races, colors, nationalities, religions and I think we are all people. If we take the time to speak with them, we discover that everyone has the same basic human values. Everyone wants to be happy and nobody wishes to suffer. Therefore all of us should try to be kind and have a good heart. Do you understand? What I am saying is not difficult to understand, is it? Do you follow me? Be kind people. You have come here to Bodh Gaya and have been receiving Dharma teachings from the Dalai Lama. This is my main message, be kind people. So now perk up our ears like rabbits and listen to the teachings of "The Three Principal Paths" by Je Tsong-Khapa.

He was born in Amdo and went to study with many teachers in the central Tibetan provinces of U-Tzang. He studied both sutra and tantra and became completely realized. He wrote 18 volumes of teachings which are excellent, drawing sources widely from the various Indian texts and commentaries. This specific text was directed to one of his closest disciples, Ngawang Dragpa.

There is a slight difference in Je Tsong-Khapa's style of teaching in these "Three Principal Paths" and in the "Lamrim" or "Graded Path." Here, in the former, the explanation of renunciation is in two parts. The first is to turn away from our obsessions with this life through remembering the precious human rebirth and impermanence, and the second is to turn away from our obsession with future lives by remembering the suffering nature of cyclic existence. There is little emphasis on taking refuge. In the "Lamrim", on the other hand, there is the discussion of the three levels of motivation. Since being a person of initial scope is the basis for the higher levels, there is first the development of interest to benefit future lives and within this context are included the teachings on taking refuge. There is a slight difference then, isn't there? Let us start the text.

"I prostrate to my Venerable Lamas."

The word "Venerable" in Tibetan is "Jetzun," which has the connotation of someone who has turned his back on all things of cyclic existence and is faced totally towards Liberation. "Lama" means a superior person in the sense of someone who has both Bodhichitta and the understanding of Voidness, which brings him to a superior or supreme state of Enlightenment. Here, "Venerable Lamas" refers to Je Tsong-Khapa's Gurus who taught him "Lamrim" and especially to his uncommon teacher, Manjushri.

Next is the verse of the promise to compose:

(1) "I shall try to explain, to the best of my ability, the essential meaning of all the scriptural pronouncements of the Victorious Buddhas, the path praised

> by the Buddha's Holy Offspring, and the fording passage for fortunate ones desiring Liberation."

"The essential meaning of all the scriptural pronouncements of the Victorious Buddhas" refers to renunciation, "the path praised by the Buddha's Holy Offspring" or Bodhisattvas, refers to Bodhichitta, and "the fording passage for fortunate ones desiring Liberation" is the understanding of Voidness, which brings us Liberation. Thus in the promise to compose, the author states that he will explain these three principal paths, and "to the best of my ability" means he will try to do so in as abbreviated a form as possible."

> (2) "Listen with a clear mind, O you fortunate ones, who would rely on the path pleasing to the Victorious Buddhas through being unattached to worldly pleasures and eager to make meaningful your life of liberties and endowments."

This is the request to listen well. It shows the type of motivation we should have when hearing these teachings. "The path pleasing to the Victorious Buddhas" is one with no mistakes and which is complete, with nothing missing. When we follow such an unmistaken and complete path, this pleases the Buddhas.

The actual explanation of the main body of the text is divided into three—the explanation of renunciation, Bodhichitta and the correct view of Voidness, the three of which constitute graded stages of understanding. The stronger our renunciation of the so-called good things of cyclic existence, the stronger will be our compassion for others. In Indian railway stations, for instance, we see blind men, people missing limbs, beggars and so forth, and it is relatively easy to develop compassion for them. But if we have no renunciation, then when we arrive, for instance, in a big city, then instead of compassion we just feel jealous of the things we see or proud of what we have. On the other hand, if we are familiar with renunciation, with the idea of how the so-called good things of cyclic existence are ultimately meaningless, then when we go to a place like New York, for instance, and see all these people, our first thought will instinctively be to feel compassion for them.

Renunciation has two directions of looking. On the one hand, with such an attitude we look down at the suffering of cyclic existence and, with no interest in it, we feel disgust and the wish to be rid of it completely. On the other hand, we look up at liberation and wish to attain it. Thus the stronger this two-fold attitude is, the stronger will be our Bodhichitta, which similarly has two directions of looking, both up and down. Then on the basis of these, if we have a correct view of Voidness, we will be able to attain either Liberation or Enlightenment.

This correct view is in terms of the two levels of truth, which follow from the Four Noble Truths. The Buddha, who is our source of refuge, taught the Dharma with his speech and specifically he taught the Four Truths and the Two Truths which are non-fallacious, they are never false.

So it is important to understand and realize them. With Bodhichitta, an understanding of Voidness brings us Omniscience. If it is only with renunciation then it brings us Liberation. Therefore here in the text the discussion is first of renunciation.

> (3) "Since working with keen interest for the pleasurable fruits of the ocean of worldly existence while lacking a pure renunciation is no method for (attaining) the peace of Liberation, in fact by craving what is worldly, embodied beings are completely bound, first we should strive for renunciation."

The phrase "pure renunciation" is mentioned here. It must be pure in the sense of being totally disinterested in the glories or so-called good things of cyclic existence. If we lack such pure renunciation and are totally obsessed with worldly concerns, there is no way to attain Liberation. If we have desire and attachment, then no matter how much good karma we might have, we will not be able to cut through cyclic existence. Therefore we must develop renunciation. How to develop it?

> (4) "By accustoming our mind that there is no time to waste when a life of liberty and endowments is so difficult to find, we will turn from our obsession with only this life. By thinking over and again about the sufferings of cyclic existence and that the law of cause and effect is never false, we will turn from our obsession with future lives."

We should think about the precious human rebirth that we have with its liberties and endowments, and also about the fact that we will lose it, for it is impermanent, and how death will come. In this way we will realize how rare the opportunity is we have now, and how we cannot afford to waste any time. This is how to turn our interest from being only in this life. As for the liberties and endowments and the teachings on impermanence and death, these have been discussed already these last few days in the "Thirty-Seven Bodhisattva Practices."

Concerning death and impermanence, however, there are various points upon which to meditate, such as the facts that death is certain, while the time it will come is completely uncertain. Death can happen at any moment and except for the Dharma nothing else is of help when it does. If we do not do something now about our forthcoming death and future lives, this will not do at all. The more we think of death like this, the more we will lessen our obsession with just this life alone.

Next we should think about the infallibility of the law of cause and effect. To understand cause and effect in all its details is one of the hardest things, but in a simple form, from good comes good, from bad comes bad. Karma is certain. From good actions happiness is certain to result. From bad, suffering is certain to happen sooner or later. So if we have the causes for suffering on our mindstream, how can we rest content and be at ease? It is like a time bomb, it is just a matter of time, for it is sure to go off. If we do not remove this cause, we can never rest at peace. In this way then we develop the strong wish to remove all causes of suffering when we think carefully about cause and effect.

At different times we experience the sufferings of birth, death, old age and sickness. No matter how much medicine we take we cannot cure old age and we cannot prevent ourselves from ever becoming sick at all. The sufferings of birth, sickness, old age and death have their sources in the fact that we have a body that undergoes birth, sickness, old age and death. This body is a mass of contaminated aggregates, in other words we receive it contaminated with karma and delusions. If we do not rid ourselves of its ultimate cause, we will always have suffering. Our bodies are a mass of conflicting, contradictory forces. Consider for instance the forces of heat and cold in the body. If we have a fever we take a cooling medicine and if we take too much then we contract a cold type of disease. If we take a warming medicine to cure ourselves of this chill, and we take too much, then again we tip the scales and have a heat disease. It is only when we have a balance of the heat and cold forces in our body that then, temporarily, we can say we are healthy. But this never lasts. It is very precarious and at the slightest jolt the balance is upset. This is pointed out in Aryadeva's text "Chatuhshataka" or "The Four Hundred Stanzas." It says there that the body is a vessel of contradictory, mutually opposing forces and thus can only bring about suffering.

We think that this body is so beautiful, but we should dissect it in our mind and look at each part separately, such as the head, for instance, or a strand of hair with a little bulb at the bottom. Look at an ear, look at an eye just by itself, look at a piece of skin, look at a heart, look at lungs. They are all disgusting and not pretty at all. The same is true regarding what comes from this body—urine, faeces, snot and so on. We see these on the ground when we are walking around and we hold our nose to protect ourselves from them. But where did these objectionable substances come from? They have not grown out of the ground, they came from our body.

How can our body be clean, it is just a source of filth. Our body came from our parents' sperm and egg, but if we were to take these substances and put them on a table in front of us and look at them, any person would feel revolted. But we are so attached to them because they become the source of the physical substance of our body, yet they themselves are nauseating. If we have lived for forty years, for instance, think of all the food that we have eaten in those forty long years on one side and then all the faeces and urine our body has turned them into on the other. How can this body be clean if it does such kind of work? We must therefore abandon attachment for such a body. It comes from karma and delusions which bring only suffering. If we exhaust or eliminate the karma and delusions we will never again take on contaminated aggregates or suffer. Delusions come from superstitions and misconceptions which all arise from the ignorance of regarding things as being inherently existent. If we realize that everything lacks such existence, our delusions dissolve and are exhausted in the sphere of Voidness. So this is what we need.

> (5) "When, by accustoming ourselves in this way, we never generate even for a moment a mind that aspires for the good things of cyclic existence and we develop the attitude with which we work day and night with keen interest always for Liberation, at that time we have generated renunciation."

Thus we must develop renunciation. Next we need Bodhichitta, an Enlightened Motive.

> (6) "But since even this renunciation, if it is not held by a pure generation of an Enlightened Motive of Bodhichitta, will not become a cause for the sublime Bliss of unsurpassable Enlightenment, those with sense would generate a supreme Enlightened Motive."

As we have said before, if we lack Bodhichitta we cannot attain Enlightenment.

> (7-8) "Carried by the currents of the four violent rivers, tied by the tight fetters of karmic actions hard to reverse, thrown into an iron-mesh pit of grasping for true identities, completely enshrouded in the heavy gloom of the darkness of ignorance, unrelentlessly tormented by the three sufferings, life after life in limitless worldly existence--we should generate a supreme Enlightened Motive by having thought about the condition of our mothers, who have found themselves in situations like these."

"Carried by the currents of the four violent rivers" refers to the four sufferings of birth, death, old age and sickness. We are "tied by the tight fetters" of black karmic debts which are something that are sure to ripen and we are in "an iron-mesh pit" of ignorance, and "in the heavy gloom of the darkness" of not seeing the true nature of reality. Both persons and phenomena seem to be inherently existent, but they do not exist in that way at all. We have a stream of changing aggregates and the mere "I" is something labelled on that changing stream as its base. But out of ignorance we grasp at that "I", which is labelled on a mass of changing phenomena, and we misconceive it to be permanent, static and inherently findable and real. The darkness of this ignorance then causes us to accumulate many black karmic debts that throw us in an iron-mesh pit of karma and we are tied by the fetters of this karma and our delusions. As a result we naturally experience the three sufferings life after life, as it says here. These are the sufferings of suffering, change and extensiveness. Since this is the condition of all our mothers as well, we must work to help them by generating a Bodhichitta motivation.

Next concerns Voidness:

> (9) "Even if we have accustomed ourselves to renunciation and an Enlightened Motive of Bodhichitta, still if we lack the discriminating awareness that comprehends the abiding nature of reality, we will be unable to sever the root of our worldly existence. We should therefore make efforts in the methods for comprehending dependent arising."

Je Tsong-Khapa's main point is for Voidness to arise in the meaning of dependent arising and for dependent arising to come about in the meaning of Voidness. Thus, we must make efforts in the methods for comprehending Voidness as dependent arising. How to do this?

> (10) "Anyone who has seen that the law of cause and effect regarding all phenomena of cyclic existence and Nirvana beyond is never false, and has had fall apart the sustaining supports of his (cognitions) aimed (at inherent existence), whatever they might have been, has entered upon the path pleasing to the Buddhas."

All phenomena of Samsara and Nirvana come about through cause and effect. This is never false. When we understand this and, in addition, have the underlying, sustaining support of our aiming at true existence fall apart, then we have entered the path pleasing to the Buddhas. When we understand Voidness we will no longer have cognitions aimed at inherent existence. In this way the basis for these mistaken cognitions to arise, their sustaining support which is our grasping for inherent existence, will have fallen apart or disappeared.

> (11) " So long as we have the separate appearance of the two understandings, that the fact that appearances are dependent arisings is never false and that Voidness is free from assertions (of any mode of inherent existence), we have still not comprehended the Sage Buddha's intention."

When we understand Voidness we see there is nothing at which we can point a finger and say this is this object. All things are unfindable on ultimate analysis. Yet on the other hand we see that things are mere appearances. But to think that these two are completely separate, unrelated insights--things being unfindable on the one hand and yet only appearances on the other--is not the Buddha's intention concerning Voidness and the two levels of truth.

> (12) "When, not in alternation, but as an integrated whole, our certitude from the very mere sight of the law of dependent arisings being never false causes all our ways of taking objects (as inherently existent) to fall apart, we have then completed analysis of the correct view."

What we need then is to see that because things are dependent arisings, because appearances depend on causes and circumstances to arise, they are void of inherent existence, they are void of independent existence. The fact that they can arise dependent on causes and circumstances is simply because they are void of existing independently. Thus, the stronger our understanding and conviction is that things are dependent arisings, that things depend on cause and effect, the stronger our understanding and conviction will be that things are void of independent, inherent existence, and vice versa. To understand these two simultaneously in conjunction like this means we have completed the correct analysis of Voidness.

> (13) "Furthermore, when we know how the fact of appearance eliminates the extreme of inherent existence and the fact of Voidness eliminates the extreme of total non-existence and how Voidness dawns as cause and effect, we will never be stolen away by views that hold to extremes."

Often we find it explained that the fact of appearance eliminates the extreme of total non-existence, things are not totally non-existent because they do appear. And also the fact of Voidness eliminates the extreme of true existence; things are not truly existent because they are void of existing in that way. But here we have an opposite way of asserting it. The fact of appearance eliminates the extreme of inherent existence. This is because, for things to appear, they must be void of inherent existence. They must be dependent arisings. Therefore the fact that they do appear eliminates the possibility that they could exist inherently. Furthermore, the fact of Voidness eliminates the extreme of total non-existence. The fact that something is void of inherent existence means that it can appear by dependent arising and that it could not possibly be totally non-existent. Therefore the fact of Voidness eliminates the extreme of total non-existence. This is the special way of assertion of Je Tsong-Khapa and it accords with the commentaries to his "Praises of Dependent Arising" by Choney Rinpoche. Thus this understanding of things being void of inherent existence because they are dependent arisings, and that things are dependent arisings because they are void of inherent existence, prevents us from falling to either of the two extremes of grasping at true, inherent existence or at total non-existence.

Next is the injunction to practice:

> (14) "When we ourselves have had insight into the points of these three principal aspects of the path, we should then rely on solitude and, by generating the power of joyous effort, quickly realize our immemorial goal, my child."

When we have gained insight into renunciation, Bodhichitta and Voidness, through the power of hearing correct teachings on them and then thinking about and analyzing them until we gain conviction in their meaning, we should then live in solitude and devote ourselves single-pointedly to meditating on and realizing them. This we should do with great joyous effort as the famous masters of the past have done, for instance the well known Milarepa, the great Gyalwa Ensapa and his spiritual sons, Khedup Sangyay and so on. Then we can reach the immemorial goal of Enlightenment. "My son" here refers to Je Tsong-Khapa's close disciple, Ngawang Dragpa, whom we mentioned before.

This concludes the short commentary on "The Three Principal Paths." It is a very important text and has included in it the essence of the complete sutra and the heart of the tantra paths. The teachings on Voidness are a bit tough, aren't they? Unless we are very familiar with the technical terms then when it speaks of the correct view, the two truths, Voidness and so on, it may be confusing. There are the distinctive ways of defining and asserting these terms in the four Indian schools of philosophical tenets of the sutras and also in the four classes of tantra. Also there is a different way of defining them in the four different traditions of Buddhism in Tibet in their own specific contexts and systems. We should try to understand them all so that we know the implications of the terms according to their context and we do not become confused. Just to know one system and then to criticize the others simply because they are different and we do not understand them in their own terms is very destructive. As it says in the "Precious Garland" and also in "Guide to Bodhisattvas' Way of Life", in such instances it is best to remain indifferent and silent, and not to say anything.

Even within the teachings of one tradition, the Gelug for instance, there is the assertion of the understanding of Voidness according to sutra and also according to tantra. There is no difference in subtlety concerning the object, Voidness, in either sutra or tantra. The difference is asserted concerning the mind that understands Voidness. Furthermore in both sutra and tantra there are different definitions and explanations of conventional and ultimate truths and the way to meditate on these two. Even within the anuttarayoga class of tantra, there are various systems which have their differences. For instance there are the methods outlined in the Guhyasamaja which are quite different from those in the Kalachakra teachings. Also we find differences in the ways of doing analytic and formal meditation. If we have not studied all these systems we will become very confused.

In short, if we do not know anything about a certain system, we should not say anything about it and certainly not criticize. Only on a non-partisan basis will we be able to appreciate the full scope of the Buddha's teachings.

The Eight Verses on the Training of the Mind

By Geshe Langri Thangpa

Translated by Geshe Rabten, Gonsar Tenzin Khedup and Lobsang Kalden

With the determination of accomplishing the highest welfare for all sentient beings, who excel even the wish-granting Gem (Cintamani), may I at all times hold them dear!

Whenever I associate with someone may I think myself the lowest among all and hold the other supreme in the depth of my heart!

In all actions may I search into my mind, and as soon as Klesa arises, endangering myself and others, may I firmly face and avert it!

When I see beings of wicked nature, pressed by violent sin and affliction, may I hold these rare ones dear as if I had found a precious treasure!

When others—out of envy—treat me badly with abuse, slander and the like, may I suffer the defeat and offer the victory to others!

When the one, whom I have benefited with great hope, hurts me very badly, may I behold him as my supreme Guru!

In short may I, directly and indirectly, offer benefit and happiness to all my mothers; may I secretly take upon myself the harm and suffering of mothers!

May all this remain undefiled by the stains of keeping in view the Eight Worldly Principles; may I—by perceiving all Dharmas as illusive—unattached be delivered from the bondage of Samsara!

Commentary on Geshe Langri Thangpa's "The Eight Verses on theTraining of the Mind"

by His Holiness the XIVth Dalai Lama

Translated by Allan Wallace
Transcribed by Tashi Broger
Edited by John Blofeld and Tsepak Rigzin

The reason we have assembled here this afternoon is for the sake of Dharma. It is traditional when giving spiritual teachings and preaching the Dharma to begin by reciting some words of the Buddha and a mantra. Among the teachings of the Buddha are the Prajnaparamita teachings on the Perfection of Wisdom, in which the explicit teachings is on emptiness, the implicit on the stages of the Path of Enlightenment. From the many teachings of the Prajnaparamita sutras we shall recite the Heart Sutra. Those who have memorised it should join in the recitation and, at the same time, meditate on emptiness to the best of their ability. Those who have not memorised it should simply use the time during the recitation to meditate on emptiness, specifically recognising that emptiness is the nature of all dependent arising. If one is not able to do that, one should simply sit quietly.

This present occasion is one in which the teachings of the Buddha, generally known as the Buddhadharma, are to be taught. This is being done in conjunction with various monasteries and centres that have been founded here in the West, so many of those gathered here to receive this teaching are from those places. Because they speak many languages, there is a need for a number of translations. I am pleased that all of you have been able to come here, gathering together from many countries with many languages and so on. Among you, there are people of many nationalities, languages and religious beliefs. We shall gradually transcend all these various superficial divisions, or classifications among people. We shall find that, when we come down to essentials, we are all the same in that we are human beings.

When I shall give the following teachings, I shall be looking upon you as human beings, as human individuals, and you should be looking upon me as a human individual, for I feel that there will thus be a good person to person relationship among us all. Externally, we vary greatly that is, we look different and wear different kinds of clothing; we have different features and physical built, but inwarthendly, we are all alike in desiring happiness, joy, and freedom from suffering. The desire to attain happiness and to be free from suffering is natural and altogether right. This is one of the human rights with which we are endowed. In accordance with this attitude or desire, each of us looks for means or paths that we feel will be efficient for dispelling our own suffering and for finding happiness, we come to have confidence in certain methods, techniques or paths. This is the starting point. A wide variety of means will be employed. Some will try to get results by means of external devices, some by means of knowledge, others by trading for profit, some by means of war or killing people, some by trying to dominate their fellow beings, and others by engaging in farming. So many means will be employed for this end.

The method to be employed this afternoon, however, will be something different. What it involves is the training of the mind. It may seem quite easy as it simply involves thinking, but perhaps it will be found very difficult. I mean the mind, the consciousness. Everyone has a word for it, but it is quite difficult to recognise it, to understand it. How is it? What is the nature of the mind? Is this mind a lump of matter? Does it have weight, does it have colour? What is its nature? It is certainly something very powerful, very effective, very mighty, since any type of thought can appear to the mind, anything can be imagined by it; moreover, this consciousness directs or motivates our verbal and physical actions; it is the cause of our being subject to wholesome or unwholesome mental influences. As to these actions of body, speech and mind, among these three we speak of the mind as being the dominating one. This is the one that employs or most directly influences our speech and our body. In fact, our body and speech are manipulated and dominated by the mind. So, not to mention ultimate training of the mind in order to subdue or discipline it, it is very difficult to discipline or subdue it even briefly. Even occasional happiness, to say nothing of any lasting happiness, comes from discipline of the mind, without which happiness is not possible. For example, if one lacks inward achievement or inner contentment, then even very pleasant surroundings, a beautiful house and so on are not sufficient to make one feel happy. Whereas, if one has this inner contentment, this inner cheerfulness, then the place does not matter, one is quite content. In saying this, I am not implying that only the mind is of importance and that external affairs and the external situation are completely irrelevant; but rather that the mind and the condition it is in are very important, although external conditions are important, too.

Some of the texts speak of the three worlds, or three rounds, as being of the nature of the mind. Nevertheless, in the ultimate or highest philosophical tradition to be found within Buddhism, it is not said that everything is of the nature of mind; rather there is affirmation of the reality of external objects, external entities. However, the subjective mind and the objective world, these two, are not held to be unrelated. This being the case, both subjective and objective aspects of experience relate to the whole, which must be viewed from both these aspects namely one's mental conditions and those of the external world. Then we are able to employ the latter in relation to external objects. For example, in coming here we did not have to come on foot. We drove here in automobiles. There are many means of transport and it is excellent that we have so many; in short, we are able to employ external phenomena to our own advantage. This is excellent; but, in addition to this, we should see what can be done in terms of mind, in terms of consciousness. We should seek out and listen to techniques for establishing happiness, make them a prime object of concern, a desirable goal.

As to the inner development of the mind, involving full awareness of thought, numerous religions deal with its task, as do a number of philosophies or philosophical systems. In every religion, one finds a wide variety of techniques and, in philosophy, very varied thoughts for attainment. These involve a great many contradictions. It is almost as though when one person says white, another says black, which appears to be flat contradiction. This being quite true on the one hand, what do these many religions have in common on the other? Actually, it is largely a matter of nomenclature. What they have in common is that all of them are trying to help individual beings to gain a state of kindness and a sense of worthiness. This, in a sense, is mental development and all are striving towards the means of attaining happiness and avoiding suffering. In this sense, I feel that they are all much alike.

On this present occasion for which I have come, we are here to discuss, to learn the Buddhadharma. This is a place where the Buddhadharma has hitherto not flourished. So, as this is the first occasion, I am very pleased to have an opportunity to be with you. I feel it is a very good one. What then is to be done? We desire to get to know each other, to cultivate a mutual respect. This means it is an opportunity for Buddhists to learn something of the religions here, especially Christianity, and to see what we can learn from them regarding, for example, how to serve the poor, and to serve others in a variety of ways. We think we can benefit from them. Likewise for those following the religions of the West this is also an opportunity for them to derive some benefit from Buddhists, especially, for example, in terms of meditation, in terms of philosophy and philosophical analysis. So, in this way, there can be and will be a very beneficial mutual exchange. The present situation of the world has much to do with economics, since it has become very, very small and different countries are mutually interdependent in economic matters. So they need to be able to rely heavily upon one another. I wish that the same could be true in terms of religion or spiritual integrity, that there should be interchange, mutual interdependence.

In the Buddhadharma (or Buddhism), we have different divisions or classifications, for example, in terms of way of life or practice, in terms of dealing with the quality of the mind. One could also say one finds different divisions, for example, that between Mahayana and Hinayana. Likewise one finds various other vehicles or yanas; for example, those of the Sravaka or Hearer, the Prateyeka or Solitary Realizer, and the Bodhisattvayana (for Bodhisattva Vehicle). Again, in terms of philosophy or theoretical aspects, one finds different divisions, i.e. the four philosophical systems of Vaibhasika, Sautrantrika, Cittamatra, and Madhyamika. Each of these four philosophical systems has its own particular mode of assertion pertaining to the base, that is to say basic reality. We are presented with the base, the path (i.e. spiritual path) and the result or fruit of that path. Each has its own set of assertions. The Buddhadharma contains all these various philosophical systems and vehicles; moreover, they are all graded, some are more developed, more subtle, more sophisticated than others. Despite their variations, they are the same insofar as they all lead to the full state of Enlightenment. The lower levels act as the base and foundations of the higher vehicles and philosophical systems. Their relationship is like, for example, that of many rivers in one country which, coming from different places, all lead into the one ocean.

The philosophical systems, such as Cittamatra, Madhyamika and so on, all originated in India. Now one also has different spiritual lines in Tibet; for example, the Nyingmapa, Kagyupa, Sakyapa and Gelukpa. These did not originate in India and do not relate to the various philosophical systems. They did not arise in India, but gradually took form in Tibet as a result of growth in different places, or of different teachers coming at various times to preach in Tibet. Hence these various lineages do not have a special relationship with any of the philosophical schools of thought or with the Mahayana or Hinayana. Thus, the four main Tibetan spiritual lineages all hold as their central philosophy that of the Madhyamika, especially the Prasangika philosophical system, and likewise share the philosophical system elaborated upon by Nagarjuna, as well as common practices and ways of life. The emphasis of all four lineages is equally on Bodhicitta. The awakening mind or Bodhicitta is the focal point of their practice. Taking the Bodhisattva way as their common path, all of them without exception also follow the extraordinary path of tantra, thus bringing about a union of the Bodhisattva or common path, and the extraordinary path. In this, all four of the Tibetan spiritual traditions are alike. There is a common mistaken notion that the different colours or types of hat worn by each lineage imply some fundamental differences among them. That is not so. Among the four lineages, the highest path of the Nyingma is called Dzogchen, the great perfection or the great completion. The Sakya call it the Union of the Clear and Void. The Kagyu call it Mahamudra.

The Geluk place emphasis upon the stages of Clear Light. Although these are different names, if one really knows to investigate them, he finds they all mean the same thing.

Now, as to the philosophical systems and different vehicles which originated in India, we speak specifically in terms of the Prasangika Madhyamika system. Nagarjuna stressed the importance of having this as the basis of one's practice and of correctly understanding the Two Truths on the basis of this system. This involves the union of the method and wisdom. It implies also the accumulation of physical and mental merits finally culminating in attainment of the full Enlightenment of Buddhahood, in which one attains the physical body which responds to the needs of others and the truth body which equates with the mind of the Buddha, especially in relation to self concern. Now in terms of this spiritual path, which is based upon the realisation of the two levels of truth, this involves both method and wisdom. Of first importance is wisdom, the very root of which is the understanding of emptiness, so it requires a vast accumulation of mental merits. As to the method aspect, this again emphasises two alternative practices in union; the essence of this is the awakening of the mind and attainment of Bodhicitta, which leads to cherishing others more than oneself. Such is the essence of the method, which relates strongly to the accumulation of physical merit.

In this regard, I shall give the teachings on the form of mental training as contained in "The Eight Verses on the Training of Mind". This text was composed by Geshe Lhangri Thangpa. In Tibet, there were two periods of the flourishing of the Dharma. They were instituted by many highly qualified spiritual masters from India. These included the great master Atisha (Dipamkara), whose arrival in Tibet caused the teaching to flourish there. From his lineage sprang the great Geshe Lhangri Thangpa, who composed this text. In the first seven of these eight verses on training the mind, what is discussed is the conventional awakening of the mind, known as conventional Bodhicitta. In the final verse there is a very brief reference to the alternative form of Bodhicitta, i.e. the ultimate Bodhicitta.

The first of these eight verse runs: "Those with determination to accomplish the highest welfare of sentient beings, who excel even the Wish-Fulfilling Gem—may I at all times hold them dear!"What is being spoken of here is the relationship between self and others. What is the usual situation in this regard? In general one can say that one cherishes, of course with high regard, one's own self, one's own concerns, and therefore the task of achieving one's own welfare by finding happiness and avoiding suffering. This burden is borne by oneself as the person chiefly concerned. At the same time, concern for others is generally discarded, as being of little importance, or even insignificant. This situation needs to be changed by undertaking the mental training which reverses this attitude of paying high regard to one's own welfare and thinking of other people's welfare as insignificant. What is to be done is to develop a high regard and great concern for the welfare of others, meanwhile looking on one's own welfare as relatively insignificant. So this is the objective. In order to accomplish it, one requires a sustained mental training involving a number of different methods.

I shall not have the time to give a very elaborate or precise explanation of this. However, if one desires to put it into practice, this can eventually be done by studying a teaching of which I will give a very synthesized and brief explanation taken from the appropriate texts. First of all is a text by Nagarjuna called "The Jewel Garland". There is an even clearer text in Shantideva's "Guide to the Bodhisattva's Way of Life". From these we learn that all of us are the same in our desire to find happiness and avoid suffering. As regards our right to these we are completely equal even in accordance with the law. So, as to our being worthy of being free from suffering and finding happiness, there is absolutely no distinction or difference between oneself and others. It is the same for all.

Similarly, we are all seemingly endowed with what is called a conceptional "I" or conventional "I" that wishes for happiness and freedom from suffering for itself. In terms of this spontaneous desire for one's own welfare, we are completely equal. Likewise, in general our worthiness to attain this happiness and be free from suffering is exactly the same for us all. So, too, is our potential for achieving that happy state the same for all. But, in terms of magnitude, the welfare of others is enormously more important. From this point of view, others are much more to be cherished than oneself. This is so, even though in these various ways we are really the same; for, despite all those aspects of sameness, I am just one person, whereas others are infinite in number. If one is really objective about this, it is quite clear.

For example, in commerce, if it is a matter of money, as to the importance of one or many sums, there is no question. Also in many other situations in which all other factors are equal, if there is a choice between one and many, naturally the many will be regarded as much more important. Now, if one should disregard infinite numbers and concern oneself exclusively with one individual, would this be wrong? On the other hand, if one should disregard oneself and be concerned with many, would this be wrong? Obviously, the latter would be realistic. That would be the authentic approach, whereas disregarding infinite sentient beings or exploiting infinite sentient beings out of concern for oneself would be both unrealistic and improper.

Now, instead of meditating upon some terrifically impressive meditational deity, we should now meditate upon ourselves, investigating within. Let us first of all visualize an infinite number of sentient beings to our right and hundreds of sentient beings to our left, with ourself in the middle. If we are unbiased, what shall we do? Shall we disregard all those people and be concerned only about our own self, or shall we disregard our self and concern ourselves with these myriads? Again, imagining our own self as just one person on the right and these myriads on our left, let us do what is normal, i.e. think in terms of the majority (as when voting) and decide what is to be done. We have put this in the context of democracy, which is a superb thing. In deciding whether to align himself with just one or with millions, any person with common sense will have no problem in coming to a decision to choose the many. If he looks at this with an objective, clear, unbiased mind, he will find how wrong he was to just cherish himself, as he has done until now. Hitherto, we have been regarding our own welfare as supremely important. This attitude is unworthy, unrealistic; it is improper, it is in every way degraded, something to be abandoned! This is quite clear. But now and then on the other hand, if one adopts an attitude of cherishing instead, perhaps by instinct, these myriads of people, that is something authentic, that is worthy. Such a person has a valuable mind, a noble mind. This is something to be cultivated on the basis of the verse from Geshe Lhangri Thangpa. The regard of regarding should be extended to all sentient beings. Instead of regarding them as being of minor consequence, no importance, no value, we should rather regard them as supreme, like the Wish-Fulfilling Gem. We should cultivate this wish to cherish others, to turn away from the selfish disregard for them which one has had until now, and long to cherish others as beings of supreme value.

The second verse of the text says: "Whenever I associate with others, may I think of myself as the lowest among all, and of the others as supreme, thinking thus from the depth of my heart." Now the content of this line is in contrast with our previous attitude of looking down upon others. Rather we are now looking up to all sentient beings or thinking of them as our own brothers, while regarding oneself as inferior to them.

We are now cherishing them and devoting our body, mind and entire being to the welfare of others, dedicating our self to the welfare of all the creatures, now viewed as supreme.

The third verse runs: "In all actions, may I search into my mind and, as soon as kleshas or mental distortions arise, thus endangering myself and others, may I firmly face and avert them." In seeking to cultivate this attitude of cherishing others from the position of one who regards himself looking up to them one finds that this attitude is incompatible with various mental distortion, i.e. the mental distortions that hitherto prevented us from escaping from self-love, prevented us from escaping from a false conception of self. In view of this incompatibility, the verse stresses that we must guard against such mental distortions. When they arise in the mind, one must keep guard on one's thoughts as if one were guarding a house. This is to be done with mindfulness and discriminating awareness. These two are like inner watchers of the mind, resembling internal police; if these are present in the mind, then external police are not necessary for one will not engage in unwholesome, harmful actions. However, if these inner guards, these inner police of mindfulness and discriminating awareness are missing, no matter how many police you have outside, they will not be able to handle it. For example, we can see from the case of terrorists how ineffective the police can be.

This same verse teaches us to recognise mental distortions as dangers to oneself and others to be firmly faced and fought. What is implied here is that, when one is investigating or keeping guard on the mind, he will now and then see mental distortions, such as attachment and anger, arise and how they start to disrupt the mind as soon as they arise, meanwhile increasing in strength. At that time, remembering the disadvantages of these mental distortions and what effect they have upon oneself and others, one turns away from them. Otherwise, one loses peace and content of mind, one loses reason and rationality, one loses balance and all goodness of mind. Among the various mental distortions, one finds, for example, anger, attachment, jealousy, pride, doubt, ignorance and so on. There are six primary mental distortions and twenty secondary ones, so there is a wide variety; but now that one is seeking to cultivate the mind to be of service to others one finds that among them is one type that is especially destructive. The ones we must be most concerned to face and avert are anger and hatred, for these are violent, malicious; they have unfortunate and harmful effects upon others, besides completely robbing oneself of inner contentment, happiness, and equilibrium of mind. Whoever says: "O! Today I am so happy because I am angry! It has given me such good thoughts," or something like that? In hospital, does any physician or doctor say, "Oh, you have this ailment, and in order to get well, you must get angry that would be very helpful for you"? One finds that anger has only destructive effects.

The fourth verse says: "When I see beings of evil nature oppressed by violent distortions, may they be as dear to me as if I had found a precious treasure." This verse refers especially to beings that are somehow extremely disgusting, such as man-eaters or very evil beings. On meeting such beings, although we may not have any desire to harm them, we may very well have a natural inclination to try to avoid them, to avert our eyes, to have no contact with them. This attitude, however, should be dispelled. What is to be cultivated, whether they are present or absent, is an affectionate concern for such beings, so that when we meet them, we do not feel, "Oh! Now shall I have to do something about them, here is a burden I must take on, or here is some action I must take." Rather, on encountering such beings, one should feel as if one had found a precious jewel, or a treasure, or something very glorious, and accept this opportunity to help them very eagerly.

The fifth verse says: "When others are angry or mistreat me with abuse, slander and the like, may I suffer defeat and offer the victory to them." Hence it is important to cultivate this attitude of being of service, this wish to cherish others, but especially one should take as the very central point of the practice cultivation of such an attitude towards beings who, for whatever reason, have a malicious desire to harm us, whether from anger or a desire to do us down; and whether they harm us physically or simply wish us ill. One should have a special regard for beings as these, as though they were very precious. With such sentient beings, if their attitude of malice towards oneself leads to some sort of conflict, what is to be done is to accept defeat or loss for oneself and allow them the victory. This is the essence of the preceding verse.

The sixth verse says: "When one whom I have benefitted treats me very badly, may I hold him as my supreme Guru."Among the vast number of sentient beings, there may be some for whom one has made special efforts to be of service, or shown some special kindness, which would be regarded as a noble and proper type of action. It would be fitting for such a person to repay that kindness and show some concern for his benefactor, but it can happen that, when we have shown kindness to someone, he responds in a very poor and undeserved way, in which case our natural response would be to feel upset and unjustly treated. Now, what is to be done by a Bodhisattva, i.e. someone cultivating this attitude is to regard the other person as his own spiritual Guru, taking what has happened as a tremendous opportunity, and specially valuing this person as someone to be cherished. This is because he has given us a chance to cultivate patience and tolerance. It is in this way the Bodhisattva cultivates this type of mental attitude. In cultivating a desire to cherish others, the Bodhisattva does it upon the basis of patience, i.e. subduing of anger. This basis is necessary, furthermore, the more one cultivates patience, the more it provides a foundation for the cultivation of a spirit of cherishing others. Thus patience is something one can cultivate with regard to an enemy or any person ill-disposed towards oneself. When one encounters such a person, it is right to regard him as one's spiritual teacher, in the sense of a great aid to one's practice. So in the Buddhist way of life or Bodhisattva practice, in dealing with an enemy or ill-disposed person, instead of being upset, disturbed or agitated by him, one looks on him with a special affection, and even with respect as a person as truly helpful to oneself as one's own best friend. If you practice in this way, then what happens, what is the result? First of all, a prime cause of being unhappy is having enemies or ill-wishers; but now, instead of being upset or agitated by them, we regard them with affection or gratitude, thinking of their behaviour as a kindness. With this attitude, one simply removes the basis for the unhappiness which normally arises in such a situation. I have just given you some precious advice, but it is quite likely that some people will regard it as unrealistic. As I have said earlier, this matter of training the mind, changing it, developing it is difficult. Yet, perhaps something can be done. Although my own practices are not so great, nevertheless I am practising the Dharma and, as a result, I have found that it is possible to bring about a transformation of the mind. Now, what should we do if we do not have much confidence or conviction about a practice? I encourage you to try it out, to check up the progress made in one month, one year. We need to make the effort and really experiment for ourselves to see whether it is possible. I have found from my own practice that it is indeed possible to bring about a transformation of the mind. The reason for this is that all impermanent phenomena, all conditioned phenomena, do not remain as static entities, but rather on account of natural inner process are forever changing. The discourse up to now has covered the first six of the eight verses of this text.

Now, we move to the seventh verse, which runs: "In short, may I directly and indirectly offer benefit or happiness to all my mothers; may I secretly take upon myself their woes and sufferings." This is still referring to the conventional awakening mind. So now, in order for this fine attitude of cherishing others more than oneself to be developed very strongly and become fervent, it needs to arise from the roots of compassion. Compassion is what is felt by a mind that cannot bear the suffering of others and longs for them to be freed from it. Besides feeling very earnestly a compassionate concern for others, we must also develop an attitude of loving kindness in which one looks upon others' happiness and well being with a feeling of joy. These two--compassion and loving kindness--are the root from which springs the active cherishing of others more than oneself. Upon these has been built a practice called tong-len (*gtong-len*, or giving and taking) expressed by the verse: "May I offer benefit and happiness to all my mothers and take secretly upon myself their woes and suffering."

To be able actually to transfer one's happiness to others and directly take their sufferings upon oneself is something only possible on a very, very few occasions; it occurs when oneself and another individual have a very special type of relationship based on karmic affinity stemming, perhaps, from a previous life. On such occasions, it may be possible actually to cause a transference of suffering from another to oneself, but normally this is not possible. Then why does one train people to cultivate this attitude? Because it leads to attaining great strength of character, courage and enthusiasm; and this improves one's own practice of cultivating an awakening mind.

One begins the type of meditation called *tong-len* by contemplating the suffering of others, visualizing their pathetic situation, their lack of happiness and exposure of suffering, which is not only occurring now but will also occur in the future, because the karmic causes of suffering are present in them. By again and again meditating on the situation of others, one eventually reaches a very earnest and heartfelt abhorrence at the thought of their suffering. There arises a sense of urgency, a longing to do everything possible to relieve their miserable situation. Recognizing that they are subject both to present suffering and the causes of future suffering, one comes to a point at which one feels that there is nothing to be done other than to take upon oneself both the actual suffering and the causes of future suffering in other sentient beings. In this practice, first of all one gladly, enthusiastically, and without reluctance imagines oneself transferring both the suffering and its causes to oneself. Actually, this can be done with visualization, i.e. a special meditation technique, but even if one is not able to perform it, still the mind can be trained in this way. Presently, one discovers that simply taking suffering and the causes of suffering away from sentient beings is not sufficient; rather one cultivates the wish that all other sentient beings may be endowed with happiness, with plentitude, well-being.

While cultivating this wish, one undertakes the second part of this practice which is *tong* i.e. sending away. Of what? Giving away of the plenitude one may have, all the good things one thinks of as 'mine', whether mental, verbal, physical or any other type of endowment. In imagination one offers all of them to sentient beings for their welfare. This relates, of course, of loving kindness, to seeing that, while sentient beings desire to be endowed with happiness, in fact their wish is not fulfilled. So, one does it as a means of fulfilling it.

The last verse of the text says: "May all this remain undefiled by the stains of the Eight Worldly Concerns. May I, by perceiving that all the dharmas or constituents of phenomena are illusive become unattached and thus be relieved from the bondage of cyclic existence." In this final verse, the core meaning relates to the cultivation of ultimate awakening of the mind. Whereas the other seven relate directly to the types of practice, this one relates directly to the awakening of the mind. To cultivate this mind of cherishing others more than oneself can involve a great danger, because we have long been subject to mental distortions, which may interfere with one's practice of Dharma. One may be polluted with a concern for the reputation that could be won from this practice; or one may secretly desire to receive present from individuals for whom one has performed the practice. Also the thought can arise: "Oh, I am a religious person, I am a practitioner of Dharma!" This may lead to a sense of pride, of superiority to other beings, and to looking down upon them. All these kinds of mental distortion and types of attitude relating to them are very apt to afflict us. Because of this danger in cultivating this awakening of the mind, one should be especially on guard against the so-called Eight Worldly Concerns. These eight include concern for fame, praise, pleasure and gain. One must free his mind completely from these in practicing the Dharma. Cultivating this type of mind must be pure in the sense of having no concern at all for oneself, and an unmarred concern for others. This is extremely important.

In the second line of this verse, the author says: "May I, by perceiving that all constituents of phenomena are illusive, become unattached and thus be relieved from the bondage of cyclic existence." This means that we must regard all types of phenomena including, for example, other sentient beings, Enlightened Buddhas, oneself, and absolutely everything else to be found in the round of cyclic existence —be they pleasant or unpleasant, good or bad —as not existing in the manner in which they appear to us. Their normal mode of appearance leads us to apprehend that they really are what they seem, whether good or bad; that they possess an independent existence, each with a nature of its own, with independent qualities. From such a misconception arise manifold distortions, such as attachment and anger. In fact, these phenomena appear to us in a manner in which they do not in fact exist, that is to say they appear to us as though they possessed independent existence.

Because they appear to us in this way, we come to believe that we are right to apprehend them thus. This misconception of independently existing phenomena is what defeats us. This is what keeps us in suffering, keeps us subject to woe.

Certainly, there really are certain things that are good, certain things that are bad, pleasant or unpleasant. It is not unrealistic to speak to them thus. It is possible to accept that some things are good or pleasant, and that certain other things are not. This recognition is not wrong, provided that one recognizes that these qualities constantly vary and that they are all dependent in nature, i.e. interdependent upon causes and conditions coming together, in such a way that they have this conventional quality of being good or bad. It is sufficient for us to base our practice upon avoiding that which is unpleasant or bad and taking that which is good. But a very fine line divides 'good' from 'bad'. To draw this line realistically implies not thinking that goodness or badness is somehow inherent in the object itself, that it exists inherently, independently. Such terms are merely conventional. To accept them otherwise is liable to spoil one's spiritual practice.

Taking all such distinctions as merely conventional is a realistic way of apprehending phenomena. That is why the latter part of the verse speaks of perceiving all phenomena as illusive, meaning line an illusion or hallucination. Such a view is required in many context, i.e. in the context of the very subtle identity of people and all phenomena. It is expressed by the term 'emptiness'. It explains the absence of a real personal identity. It is used in a wide variety of ways, including what is being referred to here in sutras and also in the tantras. In the tantras there is a term meaning 'illusory light' or 'illusion light'. This is also used in different contexts in the sutras. Terms similar to 'illusory' are used in many contexts and in many ways, not always with the same meaning. What is meant in the present context is that phenomena do not exist in the manner in which they appear. How do they appear? They appear as if each possessed its own nature. Well, it is recognised that, although each phenomena appears to have its own nature inherently, in fact it does not exist in that way. In this sense they can be said to be like illusions or hallucinations. Now in order to let us understand all phenomena as they really are, the Prajnaparamita speaks of many divisions or types of phenomena from the very basic form up to omniscient mind and all the many varieties that lie in between those two. Regarding each of these, one has to recognise that they possess no inherent independent existence.

First of all in one's meditation one strives to realise this lack of inherent existence, meaning lack of the quality of 'own nature'; and in time one actually ascertains this to be so, thus ascertaining the emptiness of phenomena. Then, as one arises from the meditation and sees various phenomena appearing in the light of that previous realisation, by which we have actually ascertained their ultimate mode of existence, one is able to combine that realisation with the phenomena before us. Then, beholding the phenomena as they appear now and viewing them in terms of the realisation previously attained during meditation, one meditates upon this life, reflecting that, although things appear in one way, in fact their mode of existence is otherwise, since they lack inherent existence. It will thus be seen that meditation on phenomena as resembling illusion can be practical.

So, upon the basis of realising the ultimate mode of existence of phenomena one comes to realise emptiness and thus understands the actual nature of existence. Now the conventional nature of the existence of phenomena as they appear is recognised merely as names, as mere conceptual imputations. Again and again, one brings himself to this realisation through meditation, until gradually the ignorance that causes one to suppose that phenomena possess own-nature declines. It is this misconception that is held to be the root of cyclic existence. Thus, by diminishing it gradually one frees oneself from the root of rebirth. It is for this reason that our text employs the term "unattached," meaning not being attached to the misconception that phenomena has a true, inherent existence. "Unattached, may I be relieved from the bondage of cyclic existence." This concludes the brief and synthesised teachings on the text by Geshe Langri Thanpa.

Now, two further teachings relating to the above will be given. First, cherishing others more than oneself, exchanging self-concern for concern for others, while cultivating a desire to be of service to others, in other words cultivating a mind of a kindliness—all of this relates to an attitude of mind. This, then, is the *method* aspect and is derived from moral considerations. Perfectly complementary to this is the *wisdom* aspect, in which one seeks to realise that, although phenomena appear, they lack inherent existence or own nature. These two should be combined. The method or practice needs to be flavoured by this type of wisdom of understanding. Similarly, one's philosophical investigation needs to be flavoured by this method aspect of practising compassion. These two are mutually complementary. They aid each other in our attainment of a very full and rounded spiritual development. So I feel it would be very good to stop here.

I realize that the process of arranging this meeting has been very hard work for a number of people. Among those present may perhaps be some who have heard many such teachings already, and are therefore quite familiar with this one, so it may seem very ordinary to them. Others, to whom such teachings are quite new, may have found them hard and difficult to relate to. Nevertheless, despite the problems that may have been encountered, I feel that you have all been listening very carefully and paying heed to what I said, so I am very pleased and wish to thank you. I wish to add that the teachings given here today originated two-thousand-five-hundred years ago in India, but that here in the twentieth century they are equally valuable and profitable to us. The teachings and practices discussed or explained here are by no means easy, and to many people, they may possibly seem quite impractical. Nevertheless, if one seeks real lasting mental peace, I feel there is not much in the way of an alternative. A very great effort is needed among the nations of the world to bring about military disarmament. Similarly, much effort is needed likewise in order to bring about inner disarmament or mental disarmament, which cannot happen without that great effort. I shall offer prayers for your good health and for the flourishing of your spiritual practice. I am very pleased with this great opportunity to speak with you and grateful for it. As my speech had to be translated twice, some people must be feeling a bit exhausted, for which I offer my apologies.

As I have come from Tibet I feel it necessary to say something about that country, otherwise some people may have the idea that I simply fell out of an aeroplane. My land Tibet is a remote one in the proximity of the renowned, and perhaps very mysterious Himalayas. I have a great deal of affection for that bountiful land. Some of the lower areas, I think, may be similar to Switzerland, whereas some of the higher areas, for example the northern plains, are barren wild places. The country is very rich in minerals. Its population is roughly that of Switzerland, about six million. The Tibetan race has a very long history and a rich ancient culture. The physical characteristics of the Tibetan people are similar to those of mine. Originally, the religion that was most widespread and flourishing in Tibet was what is called Bonpo. Although scholars have searched for the origin of this religion, that remains unclear, but in any case, it is very ancient.

Later on the Buddhadharma (i.e. Buddhism) spread and flourished in Tibet. The scriptures of the Hinayana cannon were brought to Tibet, also the sutras or scriptures of the Mahayana cannon, and likewise the teaching of tantra or Vajrayana. This last comprises four, or we can also say six classifications, all of which were brought in completely. In countries such as Sri Lanka, Thailand and Burma, the chief religion is Hinayana Buddhism, whereas in China, for example, the Mahayana flourished, as it did later in Japan and Korea, where the tantras also either did or do exist, but it seems that only the lower ones (namely the Kriya tantra, Carya, and perhaps the Yoga tantra) flourished in those countries. The highest tantra is to be found , it seems, only in Tibet. There are complete set of all the Buddha's teachings spread and flourished. The Buddhadharma comprises lower and higher teachings, including the various philosophical systems; but only in Tibet have all of them flourished, both in terms of study and of practice or meditation. Furthermore, in Tibet, there has also been a great flourishing of other major fields of knowledge, such as religious crafts, the art of healing, the study of Sanskrit and so on. As the texts originated in India, Sanskrit was the actual language used in these various fields of knowledge, but all were translated into Tibetan and have flourished in that language. The systems or fields of knowledge found in Tibet are not the same as those found in China and elsewhere.

The staple diet of most Tibetans was tsampa or barley flour, and for the nomads it was meat, butter and cheese. Formerly, due to the climate, the majority of Tibetans, despite being Buddhists, ate meat, as many still do. Yet, being Buddhists, they naturally espouse the principle of non-violence, so naturally there is contradiction here which very often comes up in questions. As to Tibetan clothing, I feel that it is probably related to that of the Mongolians. Returning to diet, especially in the Tibetan use of vegetables, I feel there is certain mixing or drawing from the Chinese cuisine. Thus the Tibetans are in many ways quite versatile, i.e. when they find food in other countries that is delicious, they adopt it. In terms of philosophy, the Indian philosophy being very profound, they took it from India. Finally with the climate being quite cold, they found the clothing of the Mongolians highly suitable.

As to the population of Tibet, it was six million, but there can be some confusion about this, as some documents put the figure at 1.2 million, or sometimes 1.7 million. This discrepancy results from the more recent figures, which concern the population of only a part of Tibet, whereas the number I have given is the population of the entire country. Since the tragedy that overwhelmed Tibet, over a hundred and five thousand Tibetans have become refugees now outside Tibet; seventy-five thousand of them are living in India, the rest being spread over about sixteen countries. In Switzerland there about 1,300 Tibetans refugees. I wish to offer my thanks for the great help given by the Swiss people and by the Swiss organisations, such as the Swiss Red Cross, to the Tibetans. I have a very warm feeling and very warm regards towards them.

The present situation of this planet is that the economic relationship between the various nations has become very close, so that they are now very closely dependent upon one another; and it seems that, due to this closeness, the people of the world and followers of the various religions are coming into contact and forming relationships. I feel that this situation is a very good one and that, furthermore, the ultimate object in common among all the major religions of the world is to make us better and finer human beings. On this point, all the major religions will come to agree. Moreover I feel it would be very good if there were increasing opportunities for mutual exchange. For example, comparative study among the followers of the various religions could take the form of discourses or exchanges of information concerning each religion. Listening to what others have to say could lead to very good relationships among the religions and their adherents, even though they each have unique points of difference as well as much in common.

Now to give a very brief synopsis of the Buddhist religion. The Buddha first of all gave beginners teachings called the "Four Noble Truths," namely the truth of suffering, the truth as to the source of suffering, the truth regarding the cessation of suffering and the truth concerning the path to its cessation. In order to well understand these four truths, it is necessary to recognize that they are rooted in two other truths, namely relative and absolute truth. At the level of relative truth, this and that, I and other, each seems to have an independent existence of its own, but from the viewpoint of absolute truth, every object and every being is found to exist only in dependence on all other existing entities. With this perception comes the understanding of the ultimate mode of existence, namely the complete absence of independent or inherent isolated existence of anything whatsoever. This ultimate nature of phenomena is called emptiness and these two differing concepts of it are known as the conventional and the ultimate modes of phenomena. The understanding of these two truths or modes of truth forms the basis for a proper understanding of the Four Noble Truths. Now, in terms of the true nature of phenomena, one sees that they arise in dependence upon conditions and that they are completely lacking an independent existence of their own. When certain conditions come together, then phenomena arise; if these co-operative conditions do not come together, or if they should cease, then these phenomena do not exist. So this then is the process by which phenomena arise and pass away.

In giving the following explanation of the Four Noble Truths, I will do so, not in the context of one individual but rather in the context of the whole of mankind, or of this world community, this human society. So now, first of all comes the first truth, the Truth of Suffering. There is a wide variety of suffering, but now the most frightening, the most serious, is that of war. The situation of the world is one in which there is danger not only to the life of each individual, but rather to the lives of the population of this entire planet.

Next, on searching for the source of the suffering leading to tears, one finds that this source is in the mind, specifically in the mental factors and such mental distortions as attachment and anger, as well as an evil related to anger, namely jealousy. Anger, hatred and so on are the actual source of suffering. Certainly there are also external weapons, but these weapons themselves are not the source of the problem, because they need to be employed by human beings; they cannot work by themselves; and, in order for human beings to employ them, there have to be motivations. These motivations are mainly hatred and attachment, especially hatred. This is a vicious state of mind. If we have contentment, happiness or tranquility, we have inner peace. If we do not have inner or mental peace, how can we have external peace? In order to bring about inner peace, it will not do to drop atom bombs on people; in seeking the establishment of peace, one has to turn to the mind. To destroy mental defects, external weapons are of no use at all. The only way is to endeavour to control one's own mind.

Coming now to the truth of cessation of suffering, it is clear that the cessation of mental distortions such as anger and jealousy, though certainly they can be ultimately eradicated, is something to look for in the future. What can be done now is to try to foresee the future. Clear understanding of what seems likely to be our future would surely reduce such mental defects as anger. To reduce anger effectively requires that we avoid the conditions that lead to anger, such as pride and jealousy. We must try to abandon these and, on the other hand, accustom ourselves to states of mind that are incongruous with jealousy an pride. That it is possible to lessen such mental distortions is something that can be verified.

The truth of the path to the cessation of suffering has as its very root compassion. This involves developing a mind of kindliness and kind-heartedness, that is to say developing motivation towards the service and benefit of others. This is the very essence of the path to cessation of suffering. To cultivate such compassion, it is necessary to minimize the effects of such divisions among humanity as races, cultures, appearance and varying philosophical traditions. Putting aside these classifications, one becomes very much of the fact that human beings are human beings and have this great factor in common. Whether we are Easterners or Westerners, believers or non-believers, all of us are human beings, that is to say beings of the same kind. From this recognition will come a true sense of brotherhood, love for one another, more concern for others, less selfishness. These things are essential. This kind of effort is indeed difficult, but it is also worthwhile.

Once again, I would like to extend my thanks to you and I will offer prayers for your welfare.

Question: So the mind itself is the power of the man. The mind itself is not another type of phenomenon arising out of something else. Well, if the mind itself is the power of the man, is what a person thinks also due to the power of that man?

Answer: I feel I must answer your question in the following way, that is, from within the mind, there are certain conceptualizations which are irrational and unreasonable. If the mind comes under their influence or domination, falseness arises. However, there are also other types of conceptualization which are rational, being based on reason. If the mind is under the influence of these, there is no fault. The start of an actual war or battle occurs in the mind, i.e. a concept of someone as the opponent or enemy arises in the mind and the concept of facing up to that opponent is also within the mind. Here is the true battle. So here there appears to be two polarities of which one apparently is wrong. Both are nevertheless viewed at the same level of mind. I hope soon after this, there will be another question.

Question: Within the mind, there are certain negative and positive aspects, but we in the West believe also in an unconscious and a conscious mind which influences us; determining that which is to be avoided and that which is to be followed.

Answer: I feel there is indeed unknown and unmanifested mind, or one might say unconscious mind, and that within this there are both wholesome and unwholesome tendencies. However, the subject is quite complicated. It is important to have a clear understanding of the presentation and complexity of such an analysis, which involves the mind, mental factors, mental cognition, sensory cognition, conscious mind, latent mind, manifest or unmanifest mind. It is necessary to determine how all of these aspects are mutually related; otherwise, just uttering one or two sentences on the matter would involve considerable danger of misinterpretation.

Question: Are not Marxism and Buddhism mutually contradictory?

Answer: I feel that this a quite interesting point requiring investigation and research. Now, on this point I wish to comment that one's view of the matter must be made to accord with reality. It is necessary to investigate reality itself and, in doing so, to cultivate what is called an ideal cognition. Thus, it is not sufficient merely to imagine something or merely think of something conceptually. Even if one does this a hundred or thousand times, such mere thinking does not necessarily bring what one has imagined into accordance with reality. But there must be the contact with reality, contact with reality in relation to one valid cognition, and establishment of reality upon this basis. This is valid and realistic, whereas merely acting upon the basis of what one imagines or thinks does not imply that one is acting in accordance with reality. Buddhism or Buddhadharma is said to be rational and therefore relates very much to this point. I feel that, in the original Marxism, there are certainly some points which it would be very interesting to check up in relation to Buddhism, especially in its Mahayana form.

Dropping the Rain of Siddhi

A Spiritual Song on Upholding the Four Mindfulnesses Incorporated with an Instruction for Meditation on the Middle View of Emptiness

By The Seventh Dalai Lama

Translated by Tsepak Rigzin

On the immutable cushion
Of the union of the method and wisdom,
Sits the kind Guru,
The embodiment of all refuges,
A Buddha with complete abandonment
And realization is there.
Through abandoning the wrong conceptions,
Pray to Him with pure perception.
Without letting your mind wander,
Place it within faith and respect.
Without being unmindful,
Hold it within faith and respect.

In the prison of sufferings
Of the endless cyclic existence,
Wander the beings of six types,
Bereft of happiness,
The parents who have nurtured us
With kindness are there.
Through abandoning attachment and aversion,

Meditate on love and compassion.
Without letting your mind wander,
Place it within compassion.
Without being unmindful,
Hold it within compassion.
In the divine mansion of great bliss
Pleasant to feel.
Abides the divine body:
The body of oneself
With pure aggregates and elements,
A meditational deity inseparable
With three bodies is there.
Without conceiving it as ordinary,
Cultivate (divine) pride and
And vivid appearance.
Without letting your mind wander,
Place it within the profound and clear.
Without being unmindful,
Hold it within the profound and clear.

Throughout the sphere of appearing
And existing phenomena,
Pervades the space of clear light
Of suchness and ultimate,
An inexpressible real mode
Of existence is there.
Abandoning conceptual elaborations,
Look into the nature of emptiness.
Without letting your mind wander,
Place it within the suchness,
Without being unmindful
Hold it within the suchness.

At the junction of multifarious appearances
Of the six consciousnesses,

The confusion of the baseless phenomena
Of dual appearance is seen,
A feat of deceiving
Magic is there.
Without conceiving it as true,
Look into the nature of emptiness.
Without letting your mind wander,
Place it within the appearance and emptiness.
Without being unmindful,
Hold it within the appearance and emptiness.

Thus is the unique instruction which was directly given by the holy Manjushri to Tsong-Khapa, a king of Dharma. This Spiritual Song on upholding the Four Mindfulnesses, incorporated with an instruction for meditation on the View of Emptiness, was composed by the Buddhist monk Kelsang Gyatsho in order to implant the predisposition of correct view within oneself and others.

Commentary on the Seventh Dalai Lama's the "Song of Four Mindfulnesses"

by His Holiness the XIVth Dalai Lama
given in Switzerland, 1979

Translated by Allan Wallace
Transcribed by Tashi Broger
Edited by John Blofeld and Tsepak Rigzin

I am very pleased that so many of us are here and that so many guests were able to come to this Christian church in order to hear some Buddhist teachings. I thank you for coming and for giving me this opportunity.

The world situation is such that from each of the various countries come certain types of material products and different types of knowledge that are conveniently interchanged, so that they become our common possessions. I feel there is much good in this situation. A few minutes ago, while I was upstairs with the Christian fathers, we agreed that it was very good to have such contacts among the adherents of the various religions, so as to encourage mutual study and mutual interchange among followers of different faiths. When in 1973 I met the Pope, there had been a similar discussion concerning the means to bring about such exchanges among the different religions. In ancient times, not only different continents, but even different villages were so isolated that it almost seemed as if they existed independently of one another, whereas now in the twentieth century, due to improved communications, etc., it seems that the countries of the world have drawn very close together, thus affording excellent occasions for a close interchange in terms of religion and knowledge. Once again, I feel this situation is a very good one, since it almost obliges people to come in close contact with those of other cultures and religions. If one maintains a narrow-minded approach or stubborn attitude, there is danger that such interchanges may simply lead to conflict or confrontation. Whereas, if we have an open-minded attitude, then these interchanges will have beneficial results and lead various religions to adopt common aims. All of them already have one fundamental common aim, namely all of them are trying to bring about harmony, brotherhood and peace among mankind.

This afternoon I intend to speak about the "Songs of the Four Mindfulnesses". What are these four kinds of mindfulnesses? The first is the mindfulness of the View of Emptiness. The second is Mindfulness of Compassion as the Root of the Awakening of the Bodhicitta Mind. The third is Mindfulness of Your Body as a Divine Body and is related to the practice of Tantra. The fourth is Mindfulness of the Spiritual Friend or Spiritual Guide. Now, the Guru lineage or the oral lineage of this text comes from Je Tsong-Khapa, and passed on to Jetsun Sherab Senge. This text was versified by the Seventh Dalai Lama. His name was Kalsang Gyatso.

I shall forego this opportunity to explain the various divisions or classifications of Buddhism, e.g. Hinayana and Mahayana, sutra and tantra; I know that some of you already have some knowledge of this, and believe that the others, by means of gradual study, will come to understand it. Therefore I will not speak on this point now. Generally speaking, the fundamental task of the Buddhadharma or Buddhism is to bring about a wholesale transformation, a good transformation. What is to be transformed is this impure body, speech and mind, so that they become a pure body, speech and mind. This is not a chemical transformation or process, but rather it involves cessation of the causes of everything unwholesome or bad, and cultivation of all that is good or wholesome. Now, in order to bring about cessation or exhaustion of the causes of unwholesomeness and to cultivate the causes of what is whole, we have to deal with the mind. If the mind is undisciplined or untrained, it will act as a cause of what is unwholesome. When the mind is disciplined and trained, then it becomes the cause of that which is wholesome. This great distinction between having a disciplined or subdued mind and not having one is the only thing that is important. Everything else is completely irrelevant, for, indeed, everything outside the mind is nonexistent.

Although there are different philosophical assertions concerning this point, the philosophical system in accordance with the one I am now speaking of does not assert that all phenomena share the nature of the mind. it does not assert that all phenomena are mind, but rather asserts that they possess a different nature from that of mind. The wholesome and unwholesome, good and bad phenomena arise and pass away in response to certain contributing or co-operative conditions. In accordance with Buddhadharma, the fundamental conditions which determined whether those qualities arose or did not arise in the past result from whether or not the mind is disciplined. A disciplined mind will give rise to unwholesome qualities. As a result, the mind acting like the root, gives rise to wholesome or unwholesome actions, depending upon whether it is disciplined or undisciplined. Finally, wholesome actions give rise to good phenomena and unwholesome actions give rise to evil things. Generally speaking, what I now mean by the terms "good" and "bad" are respectively that which brings about well-being for oneself or others, and that which does not bring about well-being either temporarily or ultimately, but rather leads to unhappiness and misery.

Here is an illustration. A false conception of oneself starts with the appearance of oneself as a seemingly independent or self-existent entity; later one actually convinces himself of the reality of this false appearance. In dependence upon this false conception of oneself arises attachment or clinging to one's own interests, accompanied by aversion towards other people's interests. If, as a result, anger or hatred arises, this destroys whatever peace and happiness were previously in the mind. This anger or the hatred will then motivate what follows – perhaps very harsh words towards others. At the same time, one's facial expression will change, becoming dark or angry. This will bring about unhappiness in the minds of other people. Thus, specifically, as a result of one's own verbal or facial expression, a certain tenseness in the atmosphere will come about. As a result of the loss of harmony arising from this tension, hostility and even wars will follow. The first World War, the second World War and all other wars arose from the growth of a very vigorous attachment to one side and vigorous hatred towards the other. Perhaps, the Swiss people are quiet and enjoy great unanimity just because, whenever world conflict arises, you abide by the middle.

Now, to speak of the opposite situation, when one's own mind is peace and cheerful as a result of discipline, then as a result, one's speech will become very pleasant and gentle, thus causing no harm to and perhaps even benefitting others. Likewise one will be cheerful and perhaps in a mood to sing a song: one's facial expression will be tranquil. One's own tranquillity will have a good influence on others, causing a general atmosphere of calm. It follows that we should control our faulty aspects of mind and cultivate wholesome ones. Is it possible to eliminate such unwholesome and faulty qualities completely? It is difficult, but one should try. None of us can be sure that we will be leading a good and wholesome life, but it is for us to hope. In order to cultivate a peaceful mind, it is necessary to practice mind-training, specifically, with a view to helping others to cultivate loving kindness and compassion. So, this bring us to what may be called mindfulness of compassion. Now, in order to cultivate these wholesome qualities on the one hand and fully eradicate faulty conceptions or mental distortions, the fundamental method to be applied is cultivating realisation or our common identity. So we direct our minds towards the interpenetration of method and wisdom. In this practice, the method helps us to grasp wisdom, and wisdom enables us to grasp method, so they complement each other. This type of unified practice is essential to treading the path of perfection. This practice of combining method and wisdom is one which is common to the Paramitayana or way of perfection in general. But the simultaneous cultivation of wisdom and method would seem to be a special quality of tantric practice, and for this reason, we now come to the next mindfulness, relating to a divine body as taught in tantra.

In order to follow this type of practice, it is necessary to follow a teacher. What type of a teacher? In the vinaya, a teacher with a certain type of qualifications is described; in sutra, other qualifications are stated, but finally what is required is a teacher with all the qualities mentioned there, together with certain others which are described in the tantra. In accordance with the depth of his experience, it is necessary for the disciple to devote himself to a teacher having the required qualities. Hence the fourth mindfulness is Mindfulness of the Teacher. Now, in the text the first verse relates to Mindfulness of the Teacher. It reads as follows:

> "On the seat of the immutable union of method and wisdom
> Sits the kind teacher who is the entity of all the refuges,
> A Buddha who has perfect abandonment and wisdom is there.

Forsaking thought of defects, make a petition with pure perception,
Not letting your mind stray, place it within admiration and respect,
Making your attention unforgetful, maintain it within admiration and respect."

There are different practices in regard to a teacher, known as the outer, inner and secret practices. The outer practice is to visualise one's Guru in the space before one's eyes. In order to signify the immutable union between method and wisdom, one visualises him upon the cushions of the sun and moon as an object of refuge, who has perfect abandonment, and wisdom like a Buddha or fully enlightened being. So one should look upon the teacher as free from any defects or faults. Cultivate admiration and respect for the teacher, do not allow your mind to stray. So now, when speaking of looking upon the teacher as someone who is completely free from any defects, looking upon him as a Buddha, such a practice is primarily related to tantra and specifically to Anuttarayoga tantra. A fully qualified teacher according to this tantra is one who has experience of the four empowerments and such a being is a Buddha.

The next verse concerns Mindfulness of the Awakening of Altruistic Aspiration towards Highest Enlightenment. It reads as follows:

"In the prison of the suffering of limitless cyclic existence
Wander the six types of sentient beings bereft of happiness,
Fathers and mothers who protected you with kindness are there.
Forsaking desire and hatred, meditate on endearment and compassion,
Not letting your mind stray, place it within compassion,

Making your attention unforgetful, maintain it within compassion."

In the first line, what is meant by this term "cyclic existence"? It means Saṃsara in which one's own mental and physical aggregates are subject to mental distortions inherent in the nature of suffering. What type of suffering? The suffering of misery, the suffering of change and pervasive suffering. All sentient beings experience these sufferings which are limitless because, as long as the causes for cyclic existence have not been exhausted, it will go on. All sentient beings experience numberless types of suffering, limitless degrees, but all those suffering sentient beings desire happiness and do not know how to find it, and as such they are bereft of happiness. This is the same for all six types of sentient beings.

Sentient beings who wish for happiness are bereft of happiness: wishing to be free of suffering, they are still subject to suffering. Would it be fitting or proper simply to disregard them? It would be utterly improper, because since beginningless time each of these sentient beings has, at one time or another, protected us, as our father or mother, they have treated us with great kindness. So we cannot simply forsake them, but rather one should forsake attachment to one's self and aversion towards others. One must cultivate the attitude of cherishing others more than oneself. In doing this, one must meditate upon the quality of compassion in which one can no longer bear the sufferings of others. Those who attended my discourse in Tharpa Choeling a few days ago, should be familiar with the meaning of looking upon self-cherishing as faulty and have learnt how to eradicate it. They should recognise the value of cherishing others and know generally how to cultivate this state of mind and be of service to others. The teaching given at that time relates closely to what is being said now. This is the explanation of the second verse.

We shall now go onto the third verse concerning Mindfulness towards one's own body as being a Divine Body. This reads as follows:

> "In the divine mansion of great bliss, pleasant to feel,
> Abides the divine body which is your own body of pure aggregates and constituents,
> A deity with the Three Bodies inseparable is there.
> Not conceiving yourself to be ordinary, practice divine pride and vivid appearance,
> Not letting your mind stray, place it within the profound and the manifest
> Making your attention unforgetful, maintain it within the profound and the manifest."

The first line speaks of a divine mansion of great bliss, pleasant to feel. You should know that, within tantra, there are four divisions or classifications. This verse relates to Anuttarayoga tantra. It can be explained in terms of either the generation stage or completion stage, and I shall explain it in terms of the generation stage. The first four lines of the verse relate to the purity of one's abode and of all that it contains, that one employs. There are two purities referred to here. One exists in the middle of such a divine mansion which is completely immaculate. In terms of purity of your body, visualize or imagine yourself as having a divine body of pure aggregates and constituents, completely pure. Furthermore, imagine your body, speech and mind as inseparable, i.e. your body being the Emanation Body, your speech the Enjoyment Body, and your mind the Truth Body, whereas normally one's body, speech and mind are of different nature, but now one imagines these to be inseparable from and of the same nature as that of the Buddha. When we are speaking of the mind, this is conceived of as the Buddha-mind or the Truth Body. This refers to the subtle mind or *lung* (*Rlung*), subtle energy current, perhaps.

Right at the present time, we possess the requirements to bring about such a transformation, or to bring about Buddhahood, as this might be called. Abandoning the conception of being ordinary one must cultivate the divine pride, looking upon oneself as a fully enlightened being and visualizing oneself vividly as such.

What is the purpose of this? The true or ultimate refuge is called the resultant refuge. This is Buddha, viewed not as another being outside of or different from oneself but as that which one will become, following the exhaustion of the impurities of one's body, speech and mind. So this practice is the means of cultivating the requirements for one's own Buddhahood, which is one's own ultimate refuge.

Next the verse says, "Not letting your mind stray, place it within the profound and manifest." The profound here is referring to emptiness and the manifest to the visualisation of one's own body as a divine body. These two together are then said to be the union. The union of the profound and the manifest is also called the union of method and wisdom. In non-Buddhist tantras, one is taught mere visualization of oneself as a deity, whereas in Buddhist tantras one visualizes oneself in the mandala of the deity and the deity itself within this emptiness. This is a uniquely Buddhist tantric practice.

The next verse concerns Mindfulness of the View of Emptiness. There are really two verses. The first refers to the space – like meditation during the meditative equipoise, whereas the second refers to the illusion – like meditation in the post-meditational period. Here is the first of these two verse:

> "Throughout the circle of appearing and occurring
> objects of knowledge
> Pervades the space of clear light which is reality, the
> ultimate,
> An inexpressible mode of being of objects is there.

Forsaking mental fabrications, look to the entity of
immaculate emptiness
Not letting your mind stray, place it within reality,
Making your attention unforgetful, maintain it
within reality."

In speaking of the "appearing and occurring objects of knowledge" we mean every type of phenomenon, every type of entity that exists, be they good or bad, be they of the nature of cyclic existence or of the nature of Nirvana (liberation). Every one of these phenomena includes emptiness; that is to say, all types of phenomena, whatever exists, is pervaded by emptiness. That means that all phenomena are mere names, being merely imputed by conceptions and therefore lacking inherent identity, so their nature is emptiness. For this reason it is said that all phenomena are pervaded by emptiness as their ultimate mode existence, "....an inexpressible mode of being of objects is there." Why is this mode of being called inexpressible? Because phenomena do not exist in the manner in which they are apprehended or seen, they exist in another fashion and are accordingly said to be inexpressible. This is the mode of being of phenomena; individual things are merely imputed by conceptions.
In order to realise this one has, in meditation, to forsake mental fabrications or conceptualization and direct the mind to the absence of inherent existence, that is to say, direct it to this emptiness. This emptiness is called immaculate emptiness. Fixing the mind on this without letting it stray is called the space-like meditation, the space-like meditative equipoise. Furthermore, this emptiness of phenomena is not something that we have made or which occurs by the blessing of the Buddha; rather, it has existed from the moment phenomena came into existence. This already is the ultimate mode of existence, lacking all trace of inherent being.

The next and final verse relates to this illusion-like meditation after the formal meditation period and runs:

"At the cross-road of the varieties of appearances and
the six consciousnesses
Is seen the confusion of the baseless phenomena of
duality,
The illusory spectacles of a deceiving magician are
there.
Not thinking they are true, l ook to their entity of
emptiness,
Not letting your mind stray, place it within appearance and emptiness,
Making your attention unforgetful, maintain it
within appearance and emptiness."

This verse directs us to imagine first that across the road a magician is performing his acts, i.e. creating spectacles, illusions, hallucinations, in which, although no horses or elephants exist they seem real to the passer-by, to whose visual consciousness they appear. The horses and elephants are not actually there, nevertheless, one apprehends them as being there. Taking this as the illustration, we now go to the fact, which is that we have our own six consciousness, all of them polluted by ignorance, so that the phenomena appear to us as if they had inherent existence independent of the observer. In fact, from their very outset, they have never existed in that way, being merely imputed by conceptions. Nevertheless, they appear as if they were truly existent in themselves. Why? Because of the pollution of our own consciousness by the force of ignorance. In terms of the ultimate mode of existence of the phenomena, they are said to be of one flavour or completely imaginary.

When this emptiness is manifest in the form of conventional phenomena, we find divisions such as good and bad, wholesome and unwholesome, and so forth, nevertheless, the ultimate mode of phenomena has but one flavour. Previously, that is during a formal meditation, one has sought the object imputed, but having sought it, one has not found it. One has sought the inherent existence of the object, but one has not found it, and thus come to realise the absence of any inherent nature or independent existence. Having attained this realization, on rising from meditation, one looks upon phenomena as they appear to oneself, and sees that they appear as if they were truly and independently existent, however, owing to the force of one's previous realization during meditation, one recognizes that they do not exist in the manner in which they appear.

This completes the explanation of this "Song of the Four Mindfulnesses". This is an extremely concise or synthesised explanation of the practice involving the union of sutra and tantra. It is up to oneself whether or not one practices the Dharma, or any religion; it is up to oneself whether one wishes to follow Buddhist Dharma or not. However, in following the Buddhadharma of the Tibetan tradition, one seeks to bring about the union of method and wisdom, of sutra and tantra. Now our time has just run out. I must give thanks to you all.

༄༅། །རྒྱལ་སྲས་ཐོགས་མེད་ཀྱིས་མཛད་པའི་ལག་ལེན་སོ་བདུན་མ་བཞུགས་སོ།

༄༅། །ན་མོ་ལོ་ཀེ་ཤྭ་ར་ཡ། །གང་གི་ཆོས་ཀུན་འགྲོ་འོང་མེད་གཟིགས་
ཀྱང་། །འགྲོ་བའི་དོན་ལ་གཅིག་ཏུ་བརྩོན་མཛད་པ། །བླ་མ་མཆོག་དང་
སྤྱན་རས་གཟིགས་མགོན་ལ། །རྟག་ཏུ་སྒོ་གསུམ་གུས་པས་ཕྱག་འཚལ་ལོ།
།ཕན་བདེའི་འབྱུང་གནས་རྫོགས་པའི་སངས་རྒྱས་རྣམས། །དམ་ཆོས་
བསྒྲུབས་ལས་བྱུང་སྟེ་དེ་ཡང་ནི། །དེ་ཡི་ལག་ལེན་ཤེས་ལ་རག་ལས་པས།
།རྒྱལ་སྲས་རྣམས་ཀྱི་ལག་ལེན་ཤེས་པར་བྱ། །དལ་འབྱོར་གྲུ་ཆེན་རྙེད་
དཀའ་ཐོབ་དུས་འདིར། །བདག་གཞན་འཁོར་བའི་མཚོ་ལས་བསྒྲལ་བྱའི་
ཕྱིར། །ཉིན་དང་མཚན་དུ་གཡེལ་བ་མེད་པར་ནི། །ཉན་སེམས་བསྒོམ་པ་
རྒྱལ་སྲས་ལག་ལེན་ཡིན། །གཉེན་གྱི་ཕྱོགས་ལ་འདོད་ཆགས་ཆུ་ལྟར་གཡོ།
།དགྲ་ཡི་ཕྱོགས་ལ་ཞེ་སྡང་མེ་ལྟར་འབར། །བླང་དོར་བརྗེད་པའི་གཏི་མུག་
མུན་ནག་ཅན། །ཕ་ཡུལ་སྤོང་བ་རྒྱལ་སྲས་ལག་ལེན་ཡིན། །ཡུལ་ངན་
སྤངས་པས་ཉོན་མོངས་རིམ་གྱིས་འགྲིབ། །རྣམ་གཡེང་མེད་པས་དགེ་སྦྱོར་
ངང་གིས་འཕེལ། །རིག་པ་དྭངས་པས་ཆོས་ལ་ངེས་ཤེས་སྐྱེ། །དབེན་པ་
བསྟེན་པ་རྒྱལ་སྲས་ལག་ལེན་ཡིན། །ཡུན་རིང་འགྲོགས་པའི་མཛའ་བཤེས་
སོ་སོར་འབྲལ། །འབད་པས་བསྒྲུབས་པའི་ནོར་རྫས་ཤུལ་དུ་ལུས། །ལུས་
ཀྱི་མགྲོན་ཁང་རྣམ་ཤེས་མགྲོན་པོས་བོར། །ཚེ་འདི་བློས་བཏང་རྒྱལ་སྲས་

ལག་ལེན་ཡིན། །གང་དང་འགྲོགས་ན་དུག་གསུམ་འཕེལ་འགྱུར་ཞིང་།
།ཐོས་བསམ་བསྒོམ་པའི་བྱ་བ་ཉམས་འགྱུར་ལ། །བྱམས་དང་སྙིང་རྗེ་མེད་
པར་སྒྱུར་བྱེད་པའི། །གྲོགས་ངན་སྤོང་བ་རྒྱལ་སྲས་ལག་ལེན་ཡིན། །གང་
ཞིག་བསྟེན་ན་ཉེས་པ་ཟད་འགྱུར་ཞིང་། །ཡོན་ཏན་ཡར་ངོའི་ཟླ་ལྟར་འཕེལ་
འགྱུར་བའི། །བཤེས་གཉེན་དམ་པ་རང་གི་ལུས་བས་ཀྱང་། །གཅེས་
པར་འཛིན་པ་རྒྱལ་སྲས་ལག་ལེན་ཡིན། །རང་ཡང་འཁོར་བའི་བཙོན་རར་
བཅིངས་པ་ཡི། །འཇིག་རྟེན་ལྷ་ཡིས་སུ་ཞིག་བསྐྱབ་པར་ནུས། །དེ་ཕྱིར་
གང་ལ་སྐྱབས་ན་མི་བསླུ་བའི། །དཀོན་མཆོག་སྐྱབས་འགྲོ་རྒྱལ་སྲས་ལག་
ལེན་ཡིན། །ཤིན་ཏུ་བཟོད་དཀའི་ངན་སོང་སྡུག་བསྔལ་རྣམས། །སྡིག་
པའི་ལས་ཀྱི་འབྲས་བུར་ཐུབ་པས་གསུངས། །དེ་ཕྱིར་སྲོག་ལ་བབ་ཀྱང་
སྡིག་པའི་ལས། །ནམ་ཡང་མི་བྱེད་རྒྱལ་སྲས་ལག་ལེན་ཡིན། །སྲིད་གསུམ་
བདེ་བ་རྩྭ་རྩེའི་ཟིལ་པ་བཞིན། །ཡུད་ཙམ་ཞིག་གིས་འཇིག་པའི་ཆོས་ཅན་
ཡིན། །ནམ་ཡང་མི་འགྱུར་ཐར་པའི་གོ་འཕང་མཆོག། །དོན་དུ་གཉེར་བ་
རྒྱལ་སྲས་ལག་ལེན་ཡིན། །ཐོག་མེད་དུས་ནས་བདག་ལ་བརྩེ་བ་ཅན། །མ་
རྣམས་སྡུག་ན་རང་བདེས་ཅི་ཞིག་བྱ། །དེ་ཕྱིར་མཐའ་ཡས་སེམས་ཅན་
བསྒྲལ་བྱའི་ཕྱིར། །བྱང་ཆུབ་སེམས་བསྐྱེད་རྒྱལ་སྲས་ལག་ལེན་ཡིན།
།སྡུག་བསྔལ་མ་ལུས་བདག་བདེ་འདོད་ལས་བྱུང་། །རྫོགས་པའི་སངས་
རྒྱས་གཞན་ཕན་སེམས་ལས་འཁྲུངས། །དེ་ཕྱིར་བདག་བདེ་གཞན་གྱི་སྡུག་
བསྔལ་དག། །ཡང་དག་བརྗེ་བ་རྒྱལ་སྲས་ལག་ལེན་ཡིན། །སུ་དག་
འདོད་ཆེན་དབང་གིས་བདག་གི་ནོར། །ཐམས་ཅད་འཕྲོག་གམ་འཕྲོག་
ཏུ་འཇུག་ན་ཡང་། །ལུས་དང་ལོངས་སྤྱོད་དུས་གསུམ་དགེ་བ་རྣམས། །དེ་

ལ་བསྒོ་བ་རྒྱལ་སྲས་ལག་ལེན་ཡིན། །བདག་ལ་ཉེས་པ་ཅུང་ཟད་མེད་བཞིན་
དུ། །གང་དག་བདག་གི་མགོ་བོ་གཅོད་བྱེད་ནའང་། །སྙིང་རྗེའི་དབང་
གིས་དེ་ཡི་སྡིག་པ་རྣམས། བདག་ལ་ལེན་པ་རྒྱལ་སྲས་ལག་ལེན་ཡིན།
།འགའ་ཞིག་བདག་ལ་མི་སྙན་སྣ་ཚོགས་པ། །སྟོང་གསུམ་ཁྱབ་པར་སྒྲོག་
པར་བྱེད་ན་ཡང་། །བྱམས་པའི་སེམས་ཀྱིས་སླར་ཡང་དེ་ཉིད་ཀྱི། །ཡོན་
ཏན་བརྗོད་པ་རྒྱལ་སྲས་ལག་ལེན་ཡིན། །འགྲོ་མང་འདུས་པའི་དབུས་སུ་
འགའ་ཞིག་གིས། །མཚང་ནས་བྲུས་ཤིང་ཚིག་ངན་སྨྲ་ན་ཡང་། །དེ་ལ་
དགེ་བའི་བཤེས་ཀྱི་འདུ་ཤེས་ཀྱིས། །གུས་པར་འདུད་པ་རྒྱལ་སྲས་ལག་
ལེན་ཡིན། །བདག་གི་བུ་བཞིན་གཅེས་པར་བསྐྱངས་པའི་མིས། །བདག་
ལ་དགྲ་བཞིན་ལྟ་བར་བྱེད་ནའང་། །ནད་ཀྱིས་བཏབ་པའི་བུ་ལ་མ་བཞིན་
དུ། །ལྷག་པར་བརྩེ་བ་རྒྱལ་སྲས་ལག་ལེན་ཡིན། །རང་དང་མཉམ་པའམ་
དམན་པའི་སྐྱེ་བོ་ཡིས། །ང་རྒྱལ་དབང་གིས་བརྙས་ཐབས་བྱེད་ན་ཡང་།
།བླ་མ་བཞིན་དུ་གུས་པས་བདག་ཉིད་ཀྱི། །སྤྱི་བོར་ལེན་པ་རྒྱལ་སྲས་ལག་
ལེན་ཡིན། །འཚོ་བས་ཕོངས་ཤིང་རྟག་ཏུ་མི་ཡིས་བརྙས། །ཚབས་
ཆེན་ནད་དང་གདོན་གྱིས་བཏབ་ཀྱང་སླར། །འགྲོ་ཀུན་སྡིག་སྡུག་
བདག་ལ་ལེན་བྱེད་ཅིང་། །ཞུམ་པ་མེད་པ་རྒྱལ་སྲས་ལག་ལེན་ཡིན། །སྙན་
པར་གྲགས་ཤིང་འགྲོ་མང་སྤྱི་བོས་བཏུད། །རྣམ་ཐོས་བུ་ཡི་ནོར་འདྲ་ཐོབ་
གྱུར་ཀྱང་། །སྲིད་པའི་དཔལ་འབྱོར་སྙིང་པོ་མེད་གཟིགས་ནས།
།ཁེངས་པ་མེད་པ་རྒྱལ་སྲས་ལག་ལེན་ཡིན། །རང་གི་ཞེ་སྡང་དགྲ་བོ་མ་
ཐུལ་ན། །ཕྱི་རོལ་དགྲ་བོ་བཏུལ་ཞིང་འཕེལ་བར་འགྱུར། །དེ་ཕྱིར་བྱམས་
དང་སྙིང་རྗེའི་དམག་དཔུང་གིས། །རང་རྒྱུད་འདུལ་བ་རྒྱལ་སྲས་ལག་

ལེན་ཡིན། །འདོད་པའི་ཡོན་ཏན་ལན་ཚྭའི་ཆུ་དང་འདྲ། །ཇི་ཙམ་སྤྱད་
ཅིང་སྲིད་པ་འཕེལ་བར་འགྱུར། །གང་ལ་ཞེན་ཆགས་སྐྱེ་བའི་དངོས་པོ་རྣམས།
།འཕྲལ་ལ་སྤོང་བ་རྒྱལ་སྲས་ལག་ལེན་ཡིན། །ཇི་ལྟར་སྣང་བ་འདི་དག་
རང་གི་སེམས། །སེམས་ཉིད་གདོད་ནས་སྤྲོས་པའི་མཐའ་དང་བྲལ། །དེ་
ཉིད་ཤེས་ནས་གཟུང་འཛིན་མཚན་མ་རྣམས། །ཡིད་ལ་མི་བྱེད་རྒྱལ་སྲས་
ལག་ལེན་ཡིན། །ཡིད་དུ་འོང་བའི་ཡུལ་དང་འཕྲད་པ་ན། །དབྱར་གྱི་
དུས་ཀྱི་འཇའ་ཚོན་ཇི་བཞིན་དུ། །མཛེས་པར་སྣང་ཡང་བདེན་པར་མི་ལྟ་
ཞིང་། །ཞེན་ཆགས་སྤོང་བ་རྒྱལ་སྲས་ལག་ལེན་ཡིན། །སྡུག་བསྔལ་སྣ་
ཚོགས་རྨི་ལམ་བུ་ཤི་ལྟར། །འཁྲུལ་སྣང་བདེན་པར་བཟུང་བས་ཨ་ཐང་
ཆད། །དེ་ཕྱིར་མི་མཐུན་རྐྱེན་དང་འཕྲད་པའི་ཚེ། །འཁྲུལ་པར་ལྟ་བ་
རྒྱལ་སྲས་ལག་ལེན་ཡིན། །བྱང་ཆུབ་འདོད་པས་ལུས་ཀྱང་བཏང་དགོས་ན།
།ཕྱི་རོལ་དངོས་པོ་རྣམས་ལ་སྨོས་ཅི་དགོས། །དེ་ཕྱིར་ལན་དང་རྣམ་སྨིན་
མི་རེ་བའི། །སྦྱིན་པ་གཏོང་བ་རྒྱལ་སྲས་ལག་ལེན་ཡིན། །ཚུལ་ཁྲིམས་
མེད་པར་རང་དོན་མི་འགྲུབ་ན། །གཞན་དོན་སྒྲུབ་པར་འདོད་པ་གད་
མོའི་གནས། །དེ་ཕྱིར་སྲིད་པའི་འདུན་པ་མེད་པ་ཡི། །ཚུལ་ཁྲིམས་བསྲུང་
བ་རྒྱལ་སྲས་ལག་ལེན་ཡིན། །དགེ་བའི་ལོངས་སྤྱོད་འདོད་པའི་རྒྱལ་སྲས་
ལ། །གནོད་བྱེད་ཐམས་ཅད་རིན་ཆེན་གཏེར་དང་མཚུངས། །དེ་ཕྱིར་
ཀུན་ལ་ཞེ་འགྲས་མེད་པ་ཡི། །བཟོད་པ་བསྒོམ་པ་རྒྱལ་སྲས་ལག་ལེན་ཡིན།
།རང་དོན་འབའ་ཞིག་སྒྲུབ་པའི་ཉན་རང་ཡང་། །མགོ་ལ་མེ་ཤོར་བཟློག་
ལྟར་བརྩོན་མཐོང་ན། །འགྲོ་ཀུན་དོན་དུ་ཡོན་ཏན་འབྱུང་གནས་ཀྱི། །བརྩོན་
འགྲུས་རྩོམ་པ་རྒྱལ་སྲས་ལག་ལེན་ཡིན། །ཞི་གནས་རབ་ཏུ་ལྡན་པའི་

ལྷག་མཐོང་གིས། ཉོན་མོངས་རྣམ་པར་འཇོམས་པར་ཤེས་བྱས་ནས།
།གཟུགས་མེད་བཞི་ལས་ཡང་དག་འདས་པ་ཡི། བསམ་གཏན་བསྒོམ་པ་
རྒྱལ་སྲས་ལག་ལེན་ཡིན། །ཤེས་རབ་མེད་ན་ཕ་རོལ་ཕྱིན་ལྔ་ཡིས། །རྫོགས་
པའི་བྱང་ཆུབ་ཐོབ་པར་མི་ནུས་པས། །ཐབས་དང་ལྡན་ཞིང་འཁོར་གསུམ་
མི་རྟོག་པའི། །ཤེས་རབ་བསྒོམ་པ་རྒྱལ་སྲས་ལག་ལེན་ཡིན།
།རང་གིས་འཁྲུལ་པ་རང་གིས་མ་བརྟག་ན། །ཆོས་པའི་གཟུགས་ཀྱིས་ཆོས་
མིན་བྱེད་སྲིད་པས། །དེ་ཕྱིར་རྒྱུན་དུ་རང་གིས་འཁྲུལ་པ་ལ། །བརྟགས་
ནས་སྤོང་བ་རྒྱལ་སྲས་ལག་ལེན་ཡིན། །ཉོན་མོངས་དབང་གིས་རྒྱལ་སྲས་
གཞན་དག་གི །ཉེས་པ་སྒླེངས་ན་བདག་ཉིད་ཉམས་འགྱུར་བས། །ཐེག་
པ་ཆེ་ལ་ཞུགས་པའི་གང་ཟག་གི །ཉེས་པ་མི་སྨྲ་རྒྱལ་སྲས་ལག་ལེན་ཡིན།
།རྙེད་བཀུར་དབང་གིས་ཕན་ཚུན་རྩོད་འགྱུར་ཞིང་། །ཐོས་བསམ་བསྒོམ་
པའི་བྱ་བ་ཉམས་འགྱུར་བས། མཛའ་བཤེས་ཁྱིམ་དང་སྦྱིན་བདག་ཁྱིམ་
རྣམས་ལ། །ཆགས་པ་སྤོང་བ་རྒྱལ་སྲས་ལག་ལེན་ཡིན། །རྩུབ་མོའི་ཚིག་
གིས་གཞན་སེམས་འཁྲུག་འགྱུར་ཞིང་། །རྒྱལ་བའི་སྲས་ཀྱི་སྤྱོད་ཚུལ་ཉམས་
འགྱུར་བས། །དེ་ཕྱིར་གཞན་གྱི་ཡིད་དུ་མི་འོང་བའི། །ཚིག་རྩུབ་སྤོང་བ་
རྒྱལ་སྲས་ལག་ལེན་ཡིན། །ཉོན་མོངས་གོམས་ན་གཉེན་པོས་བཟློག་དཀའ་
བས། །དྲན་ཤེས་སྐྱེས་བུས་གཉེན་པོའི་མཚོན་བཟུང་ནས། །ཆགས་སོགས་
ཉོན་མོངས་དང་པོ་སྐྱེས་མ་ཐག །འབུར་འཇོམས་བྱེད་པ་རྒྱལ་སྲས་ལག་ལེན་
ཡིན། །མདོར་ན་གང་དུ་སྤྱོད་ལམ་ཅི་བྱེད་ཀྱང་། །རང་གི་སེམས་ཀྱི་
གནས་སྐབས་ཅི་འདྲ་ཞེས། །རྒྱུན་དུ་དྲན་དང་ཤེས་བཞིན་ལྡན་པ་ཡིས།
།གཞན་དོན་བསྒྲུབ་པ་རྒྱལ་སྲས་ལག་ལེན་ཡིན། །དེ་ལྟར་བརྩོན་པས་བསྒྲུབས་

པའི་དགེ་བ་རྣམས། །མཐའ་ཡས་འགྲོ་བའི་སྡུག་བསྔལ་བསལ་བྱའི་ཕྱིར།
།འཁོར་གསུམ་རྣམ་པར་དག་པའི་ཤེས་རབ་ཀྱིས། །བྱང་ཆུབ་བསྔོ་བ་རྒྱལ་
སྲས་ལག་ལེན་ཡིན། །མདོ་རྒྱུད་བསྟན་བཅོས་རྣམས་ལས་གསུངས་པའི་
དོན། །དམ་པ་རྣམས་ཀྱི་གསུང་གི་རྗེས་འབྲངས་ནས། །རྒྱལ་སྲས་རྣམས་ཀྱི་
ལག་ལེན་སུམ་ཅུ་བདུན། །རྒྱལ་སྲས་ལམ་ལ་སློབ་འདོད་དོན་དུ་བཀོད།
།བློ་གྲོས་དམན་ཞིང་སྦྱངས་པ་ཆུང་བའི་ཕྱིར། །མཁས་པ་དགྱེས་པའི་སྡེབ་
སྦྱོར་མ་མཆིས་ཏེ། །མདོ་དང་དམ་པའི་གསུང་ལ་བརྟེན་པའི་ཕྱིར། །རྒྱལ་
སྲས་ལག་ལེན་འཁྲུལ་མེད་ལེགས་པར་སེམས། །འོན་ཀྱང་རྒྱལ་སྲས་སྤྱོད་པ་
རླབས་ཆེན་རྣམས། །བློ་དམན་བདག་འདྲས་གཏིང་དཔག་དཀའ་བའི་ཕྱིར།
།འགལ་དང་མ་འབྲེལ་ལ་སོགས་ཉེས་པའི་ཚོགས། །དམ་པ་རྣམས་ཀྱི་བཟོད་
པར་མཛད་དུ་གསོལ། །དེ་ལས་བྱུང་བའི་དགེ་བས་འགྲོ་བ་ཀུན། །དོན་
དམ་ཀུན་རྫོབ་བྱང་ཆུབ་སེམས་མཆོག་གིས། །སྲིད་དང་ཞི་བའི་མཐའ་ལ་
མི་གནས་པའི། །སྤྱན་རས་གཟིགས་མགོན་དེ་དང་མཚུངས་པར་ཤོག །
ཅེས་པ་འདི་རང་གཞན་ལ་ཕན་པའི་དོན་དུ་ལུང་དང་རིགས་པ་སྨྲ་བའི་བཙུན་པ་ཐོགས་
མེད་ཀྱིས་དངུལ་ཆུའི་རིན་ཆེན་ཕུག་ཏུ་སྦྱར་བའོ།།

༄། །ལམ་གྱི་གཙོ་བོ་རྣམ་གསུམ་གྱི་རྩ་བ་བཞུགས་སོ།།

༄། །རྗེ་བཙུན་བླ་མ་རྣམས་ལ་ཕྱག་འཚལ་ལོ། །རྒྱལ་བའི་གསུང་རབ་ཀུན་གྱི་སྙིང་པོའི་དོན། །རྒྱལ་སྲས་དམ་པ་རྣམས་ཀྱིས་བསྔགས་པའི་ལམ། །སྐལ་ལྡན་ཐར་འདོད་རྣམས་ཀྱི་འཇུག་ངོགས་དེ། ཇི་ལྟར་ནུས་བཞིན་བདག་གིས་བཤད་པར་བྱ། །གང་དག་སྲིད་པའི་བདེ་ལ་མ་ཆགས་ཤིང་། །དལ་འབྱོར་དོན་ཡོད་བྱ་ཕྱིར་བརྩོན་པ་ཡིས། །རྒྱལ་བ་དགྱེས་པའི་ལམ་ལ་ཡིད་རྟོན་པའི། །སྐལ་ལྡན་དེ་དག་དང་བའི་ཡིད་ཀྱིས་ཉོན། །རྣམ་དག་ངེས་འབྱུང་མེད་པར་སྲིད་མཚོ་ཡི། །བདེ་འབྲས་དོན་གཉེར་ཞི་བའི་ཐབས་མེད་ལ། །སྲིད་ལ་བརྐམ་པ་ཡིས་ཀྱང་ལུས་ཅན་རྣམས། །ཀུན་ནས་འཆིང་ཕྱིར་ཐོག་མར་ངེས་འབྱུང་བཙལ། །དལ་འབྱོར་རྙེད་དཀའ་ཚེ་ལ་ལོང་མེད་པ། །ཡིད་ལ་གོམས་པས་ཚེ་འདིའི་སྣང་ཞེན་ལྡོག །ལས་འབྲས་མི་བསླུ་འཁོར་བའི་སྡུག་བསྔལ་རྣམས། །ཡང་ཡང་བསམ་ན་ཕྱི་མའི་སྣང་ཞེན་ལྡོག །དེ་ལྟར་གོམས་པས་འཁོར་བའི་ཕུན་ཚོགས་ལ། །ཡིད་སྨོན་སྐད་ཅིག་ཙམ་ཡང་མི་སྐྱེ་ཞིང་། །ཉིན་མཚན་ཀུན་ཏུ་ཐར་པ་དོན་གཉེར་བློ། །བྱུང་ན་དེ་ཚེ་ངེས་འབྱུང་སྐྱེས་པ་ལགས། །ངེས་འབྱུང་དེ་ཡང་རྣམ་དག་སེམས་བསྐྱེད་ཀྱིས། །ཟིན་པ་མེད་ན་བླ་མེད་བྱང་ཆུབ་ཀྱི། །ཕུན་ཚོགས་བདེ་བའི་རྒྱུ་རུ་མི་འགྱུར་བས། །བློ་ལྡན་རྣམས་ཀྱིས་བྱང་ཆུབ་སེམས་མཆོག་བསྐྱེད། །ཤུགས་དྲག་ཆུ་བོ་བཞི་ཡི་རྒྱུན་གྱིས་ཁྱེར། །བཟློག་དཀའ་ལས་ཀྱི་འཆིང་བ་དམ་པོས་བསྡམས། །བདག་འཛིན་ལྕགས་ཀྱི་

དྲ་བའི་སྦུབས་སུ་ཚུད། །མ་རིག་མུན་པའི་སྨག་ཆེན་ཀུན་ནས་འཐིབས།
།མུ་མེད་སྲིད་པར་སྐྱེ་ཞིང་སྐྱེ་བ་རུ། །སྡུག་བསྔལ་གསུམ་གྱིས་རྒྱུན་ཆད་
མེད་པར་མནར། །གནས་སྐབས་འདི་འདྲར་གྱུར་པའི་མ་རྣམས་ཀྱི། །ངང་
ཚུལ་བསམས་ནས་སེམས་མཆོག་བསྐྱེད་པར་མཛོད། །གནས་ལུགས་རྟོགས་
པའི་ཤེས་རབ་མི་ལྡན་ན། །ངེས་འབྱུང་བྱང་ཆུབ་སེམས་ལ་གོམས་བྱས་
ཀྱང་། །སྲིད་པའི་རྩ་བ་བཅད་པར་མི་ནུས་པས། །དེ་ཕྱིར་རྟེན་འབྲེལ་
རྟོགས་པའི་ཐབས་ལ་འབད། །གང་ཞིག་འཁོར་འདས་ཆོས་རྣམས་ཐམས་
ཅད་ཀྱི། །རྒྱུ་འབྲས་ནམ་ཡང་བསླུ་བ་མེད་མཐོང་ཞིང་། །དམིགས་པའི་
གཏད་སོ་གང་ཡིན་ཀུན་ཞིག་པ། །དེ་ནི་སངས་རྒྱས་དགྱེས་པའི་ལམ་ལ་
ཞུགས། །སྣང་བ་རྟེན་འབྲེལ་བསླུ་བ་མེད་པ་དང་། །སྟོང་པ་ཁས་ལེན་བྲལ་
བའི་གོ་བ་གཉིས། ཇི་སྲིད་སོ་སོར་སྣང་བ་དེ་སྲིད་དུ། །ད་དུང་ཐུབ་པའི་
དགོངས་པ་རྟོགས་པ་མེད། །ནམ་ཞིག་རེས་འཇོག་མེད་པར་ཅིག་ཅར་དུ།
།རྟེན་འབྲེལ་མི་བསླུར་མཐོང་བ་ཙམ་ཉིད་ནས། །ངེས་ཤེས་ཡུལ་གྱི་འཛིན་
སྟངས་ཀུན་འཇིག་ན། །དེ་ཚེ་ལྟ་བའི་དཔྱད་པ་རྫོགས་པ་ལགས། །གཞན་
ཡང་སྣང་བས་ཡོད་མཐའ་སེལ་བ་དང་། །སྟོང་པས་མེད་མཐའ་སེལ་ཞིང་
སྟོང་པ་ཉིད། །རྒྱུ་དང་འབྲས་བུར་འཆར་བའི་ཚུལ་ཤེས་ན། །མཐར་
འཛིན་ལྟ་བས་འཕྲོག་པར་མི་འགྱུར་རོ། །དེ་ལྟར་ལམ་གྱི་གཙོ་བོ་རྣམ་གསུམ་
གྱི། །གནད་རྣམས་རང་གིས་ཇི་བཞིན་རྟོགས་པའི་ཚེ། །དབེན་པ་བསྟེན་ཏེ་
བརྩོན་འགྲུས་སྟོབས་བསྐྱེད་ནས། །གཏན་གྱི་མདུན་མ་མྱུར་དུ་སྒྲུབས་ཤིག་
བུ། ། ཞེས་པ་འདི་ནི་མང་དུ་ཐོས་པའི་དགེ་སློང་བློ་བཟང་གྲགས་པའི་དཔལ་གྱིས་
ཚ་ཁོ་དཔོན་པོ་ངག་དབང་གྲགས་པ་ལ་གདམས་པའོ།།

༄༅། །བཀའ་གདམས་པའི་བཤེས་གཉེན་རི་ཐང་པ་རྡོ་རྗེ་
སེང་གེས་མཛད་པའི་བློ་སྦྱོང་ཚིག་
བརྒྱད་མ་བཞུགས་སོ།

༄ བདག་ནི་སེམས་ཅན་ཐམས་ཅད་ལ།།
ཡིད་བཞིན་ནོར་བུ་ལས་ལྷག་པའི།།
དོན་མཆོག་སྒྲུབ་པའི་བསམ་པ་ཡིས།།
རྟག་ཏུ་གཅེས་པར་འཛིན་པར་ཤོག །

གང་དུ་སུ་དང་འགྲོགས་པའི་ཚེ།།
བདག་ཉིད་ཀུན་ས་དམན་བལྟ་ཞིང་།།
གཞན་ལ་བསམ་པ་ཐག་པ་ཡིས།།
མཆོག་ཏུ་གཅེས་པར་འཛིན་པར་ཤོག །

སྤྱོད་ལམ་ཀུན་ཏུ་རང་རྒྱུད་ལ།།
རྟོག་ཅིང་ཉོན་མོངས་སྐྱེས་མ་ཐག །
བདག་གཞན་མ་རུངས་བྱེད་པས་ན།།
བཙན་ཐབས་གདོང་ནས་བཟློགཔར་ཤོག །

རང་བཞིན་ངན་པའི་སེམས་ཅན་ནི།།
སྡིག་སྡུག་དྲག་པོས་ནོན་མཐོང་ཚེ།།

རིན་ཆེན་གཏེར་དང་འཕྲད་པ་བཞིན།།
སྙེད་པར་དཀའ་བའི་གཅེས་འཛིན་ཤོག །

བདག་ལ་གཞན་གྱིས་ཕྲག་དོག་གིས།།
གཤེ་སྐུར་ལ་སོགས་མི་རིགས་པའི།།
གྱོང་ཁ་རང་གིས་ལེན་པ་དང་།།
རྒྱལ་ཁ་གཞན་ལ་འབུལ་བར་ཤོག །

གང་ལ་བདག་གིས་ཕན་བཏགས་པའི།།
རེ་བ་ཆེ་བ་གང་ཞིག་གིས།།
ཤིན་ཏུ་མི་རིགས་གནོད་བྱེད་ནའང་།།
བཤེས་གཉེན་དམ་པར་བལྟ་བར་ཤོག །

མདོར་ན་དངོས་དང་བརྒྱུད་པ་ཡིས།།
ཕན་བདེ་མ་རྣམས་ཀུན་ལ་འབུལ།།
མ་ཡི་གནོད་དང་སྡུག་བསྔལ་ཀུན།།
གསང་བས་བདག་ལ་ལེན་པར་ཤོག །

དེ་དག་ཀུན་ཀྱང་ཆོས་བརྒྱད་ཀྱི།།
རྟོག་པའི་དྲི་མས་མ་སྦགས་ཤིང་།།
ཆོས་ཀུན་སྒྱུ་མར་ཤེས་པའི་བློས།།
ཞེན་མེད་འཆིང་བ་ལས་གྲོལ་ཤོག །

༄༅། །དབུ་མའི་ལྟ་ཁྲིད་དྲན་པ་བཞི་ལྡན་གྱི་མགུར་དབྱངས་
དངོས་གྲུབ་ཆར་འབེབས་བཞུགས་སོ།

ༀ ཐབས་ཤེས་ཟུང་འཇུག་འགྱུར་མེད་ཀྱི་གདན་སྟེང་ན།།
སྐྱབས་ཀུན་ངོ་བོ་དྲིན་ཅན་གྱི་བླ་མ་བཞུགས།།
སྤངས་རྟོགས་རྫོགས་པའི་སངས་རྒྱས་ཤིག་དེ་ན་གདའ།།
སྐྱོན་རྟོག་སྤངས་ནས་དག་སྣང་གིས་གསོལ་བ་ཐོབ།
རང་སེམས་རྒྱ་ཡན་དུ་མ་འཇོག་མོས་གུས་ཀྱི་ངང་དུ་ཞོག།
དྲན་པ་བརྗེད་མེད་དུ་བྱས་ནས་མོས་གུས་ཀྱི་ངང་དུ་ཟུངས།
འཁོར་བ་མཐའ་མེད་སྡུག་བསྔལ་གྱི་བཙོན་ར་ན།
བདེ་བས་ཕོངས་པའི་རིགས་དྲུག་གི་སེམས་ཅན་འཁྲམས།
དྲིན་གྱིས་བསྐྱངས་པའི་ཕ་མ་རྣམས་དེ་ན་གདའ།
ཆགས་སྡང་སྤངས་ནས་གཅེས་འཛིན་དང་སྙིང་རྗེ་སྒོམས།
རང་སེམས་རྒྱ་ཡན་དུ་མ་འཇོག་སྙིང་རྗེ་ཡི་ངང་དུ་ཞོག་
དྲན་པ་བརྗེད་མེད་དུ་བྱས་ནས་སྙིང་རྗེ་ཡི་ངང་དུ་ཟུངས།
སྐྱིད་དུ་ཚོར་བ་བདེ་ཆེན་གྱི་གཞལ་ཡས་ན།
ཕུང་ཁམས་དག་པ་རང་ལུས་ཀྱི་ལྷ་སྐུ་བཞུགས།
སྐུ་གསུམ་དབྱེར་མེད་ཡི་དམ་ཞིག་དེ་ན་གདའ།
ཕལ་པར་མ་འཛིན་ང་རྒྱལ་དང་གསལ་སྣང་སྦྱོངས།
རང་སེམས་རྒྱ་ཡན་དུ་མ་འཇོག་ཟབ་གསལ་གྱི་ངང་དུ་ཞོག

དྲན་པ་བརྗེད་མེད་དུ་བྱས་ནས་ཟབ་གསལ་གྱི་ངང་དུ་ཟུངས།
སྣང་ཞིང་སྲིད་པ་ཤེས་བྱ་ཡི་དཀྱིལ་འཁོར་ན།
ཆོས་ཉིད་དོན་དམ་འོད་གསལ་གྱི་ནམ་མཁས་ཁྱབ།
བརྗོད་བྲལ་དོན་གྱི་གནས་ལུགས་ཤིག་དེ་ན་གདའ།
བློས་བྱས་སྤྲངས་ནས་སྟོང་སང་གི་ངོ་བོ་ལྟོས།
རང་སེམས་རྒྱ་ཡན་དུ་བྱས་ནས་ཆོས་ཉིད་ཟ་ཟི་མཐོང་།
བསླུ་ཁྲིད་སྒྱུ་མའི་ལྟད་མོ་ཞིག་དེ་ན་གདའ།
བདེན་ཚེ་མ་སྐམ་སྟོང་ཉིད་ཀྱི་ངོ་བོ་ལྟོས།
རང་སེམས་རྒྱ་ཡན་རུ་མ་འཇོག་སྣང་སྟོང་གི་ངང་དུ་ཟུངས།
དྲན་པ་བརྗེད་མེད་དུ་བྱས་ནས་སྣང་སྟོང་གི་ངང་དུ་ཟུངས།

དེ་ལྟར་རྗེ་བཙུན་འཇམ་དཔལ་དབྱངས་ཀྱིས་ཆོས་ཀྱི་རྒྱལ་པོ་ཙོང་ཁ་པ་ཆེན་པོར་དངོས་སུ་གནང་བའི་གདམས་ངག་ཁྲིད་པར་ཅན་དྲན་པ་བཞིན་ལྡན་གྱི་ལྷ་ཁྲིད་དང་སྦྱར་བའི་མགུར་དབྱངས་འདི་ཡང་རང་གཞན་ལ་ཡང་དག་པའི་ལྟ་བའི་བག་ཆགས་འཇོག་པའི་ཆེད་དུ་ཤཱཀྱའི་དགེ་སློང་བློ་བཟང་སྐལ་བཟང་རྒྱ་མཚོས་བསྙེབས་པའོ།